THE PAPACY
A BRIEF HISTORY

JAMES A. CORBETT

Professor of History
University of Notre Dame

AN ANVIL ORIGINAL
under the general editorship of
LOUIS L. SNYDER

D. VAN NOSTRAND COMPANY, INC.
PRINCETON, NEW JERSEY
TORONTO   LONDON
NEW YORK

TO MARY, PHILIP, AND CATHY

1. Papacy — History
2. Papacy — History — Sources

D. VAN NOSTRAND COMPANY, INC.

120 Alexander St., Princeton, New Jersey
257 Fourth Avenue, New York 10, New York
25 Hollinger Rd., Toronto 16, Canada
Macmillan & Co., Ltd., St. Martin's St.,
London, W.C. 2, England

*All correspondence should be addressed to the
principal office of the company at Princeton, N. J.*

COPYRIGHT, ©, 1956, BY
JAMES A. CORBETT
Published simultaneously in Canada by
D. VAN NOSTRAND COMPANY (Canada), LTD.

Library of Congress Catalog Card No. 56-6881

PRINTED IN THE UNITED STATES OF AMERICA

PREFACE

THE papacy is a unique institution. No other in the Western world is older; none has had greater influence in the formation of Christian civilization. None has been loved or hated so much, none so often misunderstood and reviled. It has been called the seat of anti-Christ, of usurpers and imposters, the instrument of shrewd men trying to enslave the minds of men, yet it has survived all attacks made upon it and today enjoys great prestige, respect, and influence throughout the world. Its very vitality amazes and confounds its enemies.

It was founded in a distant corner of the eastern Mediterranean when the pagan empire of Rome was at the peak of its power. The emperors of the greatest power on earth persecuted it ruthlessly and sought to stamp it out —and it survived the collapse of the Roman Empire. It lived for centuries amidst a world of barbarians—and stood firm against their brutality and ignorance. It faced the strife and disorders of the feudal world—and gave it a spiritual unity and sense for law. It encountered the national monarchies which challenged its position and power—and outlived their absolutism and the collapse of the Old Regime. It faced the hostility of the French Revolution and of Napoleon—and weathered the ordeal. It witnessed the rise of constitutional, parliamentary regimes in the nineteenth century, met their hostility or indifference—and emerged with new vitality and strength. It has met the social and economic upheavals of the Industrial Revolution with a demand for social justice. It has faced the challenge of a false liberalism, of scientific materialism, and agnosticism with a renewed intellectual and spiritual vigor of its own. It has seen in the twentieth century the rise of totalitarian states which have treated it with contempt—and has survived the collapse of three of them (Italy, Germany, Japan) while urging a society of free men governed by law. It was born in an empire when slavery was considered normal and natural—and

3

helped men to freedom from it. Today the papacy meets the new slavery, which again seems natural and normal to the strongest totalitarian state of the century—and again it meets the old challenge with the certain knowledge that "the gates of Hell shall not prevail against it."

For nearly two thousand years this institution has been the center of unity of the Catholic Church. Some two hundred and fifty men have presided over the Holy See as popes. They have been slaves and freedmen, serfs, commoners and nobles, Greeks, Romans, Syrians, French, German, and English. They have included great saints and great sinners, men of high learning and men of low repute. Some have resorted to base intrigue to reach this highest office in the Church; others, who considered themselves unworthy of such honor and responsibility, have found themselves chosen to bear its burdens. The papacy has lived through the whole drama of Western civilization, sometimes leading to great spiritual and cultural heights, at other times weakening under the pressures of the day and of human frailty; but always it has taught the same divine truths revealed to the apostles and entrusted to their care by Christ.

When and how was the papacy founded? What is its purpose and its powers? What were its achievements and failures? To answer these questions adequately would require much more space than that at our command. We can only survey briefly the high points of the complex and fascinating story.

I am deeply grateful to Father Philip Hughes, Professor of Church History at the University of Notre Dame, who read the manuscript, for his numerous suggestions and for the benefit of his vast learning. Needless to say he is in no way responsible for any errors this book may contain.

South Bend, Indiana   JAMES A. CORBETT

TABLE OF CONTENTS

Part I

THE PAPACY
A Brief History

— 1 —

THE FOUNDATION AND EARLY
PERSECUTIONS

The Primacy of Peter. The first and best source of our knowledge about the origin of the papacy is, of course, the New Testament. From it we learn that the first pope was Peter, a fisherman from Bethsaida on the left bank of the Jordan. Until he met Christ, he was called Simon, son of Jona. It was his brother Andrew who brought Simon to Christ. At this very first meeting Christ gave Simon a new name, one full of meaning for the role he was chosen to play. He renamed him *Cepha*, the Aramaic word for rock. The Greek word for rock is *petros,* whence the English Peter. The reason for giving him a new name was only made clear on another occasion before the Crucifixion when Christ said to Peter: "Thou art Peter, and it is upon this rock that I shall build my church, and the gates of hell shall not prevail against it; and I will give to thee the keys of the kingdom of heaven, and whatsoever thou shalt bind on earth shall be bound in heaven and whatsoever thou shalt loose on earth shall be loosed in heaven." In these simple but momentous words Christ singles out Peter from all the others to be the head of the Church and to have supreme power over it after Christ should have left them. The appointment was confirmed on His third appearance to the disciples after the Resurrection. Then He asked Peter three times whether he loved Him more than the other disciples. To Peter's affirmative answers Christ replied: "Feed my lambs, feed my sheep." Peter, then, was entrusted with the tremendous responsibility of teaching and caring for the whole body of the faithful. Matthew, Mark, Luke, and John never doubted the primacy which had been given to Peter: when naming the Apostles they always name Peter first.

Peter himself had no doubt of it. As the Apostles assembled in Jerusalem after the Ascension, it was Peter who presided at the election of Matthias to replace Judas. Ten days later when at Pentecost the Apostles received the gift of tongues, it was again Peter who explained to the astounded crowds how Christ had fulfilled the prophecies of the Old Testament about Him. It was Peter who, first of all the Apostles, performed a miracle by restoring a lame man to health, and who told the rulers and elders of Jerusalem by what power he had cured the cripple. It was Peter to whom the vision was given which explained that Christianity was to be for the Gentiles also, and who answered those insisting that the Gentiles be circumcised. "There was much disputing over it until Peter rose and said to them: Brethren, you know well enough how from early days it has been God's choice that the Gentiles should hear the message of the Gospel from the lips and so learn to believe."

After a number of years of preaching in the Near East, Peter went to Rome and was martyred there. These two historical facts are no longer seriously questioned by historians of the early Church. There is still, however, strong disagreement as to whether the supreme jurisdiction entrusted by Christ to Peter devolved upon his successors, the bishops of Rome.

The Church teaches, and it has always taught, that the primacy of Peter is held by all the successors of Peter. The popes, like Peter, are the vicars of Christ. Christ founded the Church and remains its true, though invisible, head. The popes, as successors of Peter, are the visible heads of the Church in this world and have the same powers and duties which Christ gave to Peter: to preserve intact the original deposit of faith entrusted to the Apostles by Christ, to teach it with authority and without error to all nations, to be the center of unity with supreme jurisdiction over the Church.

This teaching has been and remains a great stumbling block for those outside the Church. It has led historians to interpretations that differ all the way from complete acceptance to complete rejection. This does not mean that the methods of historical research are faulty, but rather that every historian has a philosophy or theology which will influence his interpretations of the documents he studies.

The historian is limited in his search for the truth not only by the great loss and destruction of documents of other ages, but by the nature of historical knowledge, its methods and limitations. History is not the only way of knowing. The philosopher and the theologian use different methods to discover truths of a different and even higher order. Their conclusions do not contradict the truths learned by the historian; rather, they complete them and give us a richer and deeper understanding of reality.

The documents which have survived indicate an almost universal acceptance in the early Church of a belief that the Bishop of Rome actually possessed supreme authority. They indicate the continuing presence of a strong tradition in favor of the primacy of Rome.

Actually, the successors of Peter did not claim a primacy, they exercised it. Before the end of the first century, Pope Clement I, who had known Peter and Paul, intervened with gentle firmness in a schism in the church of Corinth: "If some shall disobey the words which have been spoken by Him through us," Clement writes, "let them know, that they will involve themselves in no small transgression." (*See Document No. 1.*) Although St. John the Apostle was still living at Ephesus and there were other bishops closer to Corinth, it was the Bishop of Rome who exercised the right to settle the dispute. Corinth recognized the right of Rome to intervene by accepting the decision.

The letter of Bishop Ignatius of Antioch, which he wrote to the Roman church in 107 while on his way to Rome to be martyred, indicates the special position this eastern bishop recognized Rome as possessing: "Never have you envied anyone. You have been others' teachers. I trust that what you have taught and prescribed to others may now be applied to yourselves." (*See Document No. 2.*)

The pre-eminence of Rome is seen again in the book of Irenaeus, Bishop of Lyons, *Against Heretics,* written

towards the end of the second century. In this, desiring
to offer a simple means of learning with security what is
the true tradition of Christian belief, Irenaeus refers his
reader to the tradition of the Bishop of Rome, whose
succession from Peter and Paul, he says, all men know.
He adds a further reason for the security of the Roman
tradition: "With this church, on account of its greater
authority, every church must agree." (*See Document No.
3.*)

When the churches of Asia were in disagreement as
to the proper time to celebrate Easter, about the year
190, Pope Victor did not hesitate to intervene and to
excommunicate those churches that refused to follow the
Roman custom. There was a great controversy and Victor's severity was blamed. But no one questioned his
right to act. Later, in 260, Pope Dionysius condemned
the bishop of the great and ancient see of Alexandria in
Egypt, and Alexandria accepted the decision.

In this same third century, Cyprian, the Roman lawyer
who after his conversion became Bishop of Carthage,
was no doubt an independent-minded bishop, yet he
recognized Rome as the center of unity of faith. Although he disagreed with Pope Stephen on the question
of rebaptizing converts from heresy, he saw clearly the
true position of the pope in the Church.

These examples bring out the traditional teaching of
the Church and show that even in the early times there
was a widespread acceptance of the special, though un-
defined, position of the Bishop of Rome. The many
visits of outstanding Christian leaders to Rome from all
over the empire, and numerous letters of popes, condemning heresy and correcting discipline, indicate the
prestige that the papacy enjoyed. Its prominence was
recognized, not because the popes of the early centuries
had great personal merits comparable to those of a
Cyprian, an Ambrose, or an Augustine, but because the
see of Rome, no matter who held it, was founded by
Peter to whom the keys had been entrusted. To be sure,
the jurisdiction of the popes was not exercised as often
as in later centuries, but exercised it was, even though
the Church was outlawed and its heads lived in the very
city of the emperors who were determined to destroy
Christianity altogether.

The history of the popes of the first three centuries is not well known. Often forced to live in hiding, they were hunted down and martyred like other members of the Church. We have few documents which relate their lives and deeds—only occasional glimpses, sometimes only their names; but always they are acting like men conscious of their supreme authority. The see of Rome is the only one for which we have a complete list of names of the bishops.

The Persecutions. There were Christians in Rome at least by 49-50. St. Paul speaks of them in 58 as those "whose faith is so renowned throughout the world." The first persecution of the Roman Church followed the burning of Rome in 64 during the reign of Nero. Thousands of Christians were covered with pitch and turned into human torches to light the imperial gardens. Peter and Paul were the two most important victims of the emperor's sadistic madness. The death of Nero gave the Christians a respite from persecution for thirty years, during which the decimated community gradually recovered and grew in numbers. From Nero to Septimius Severus, from 64 to 193, Christianity was proscribed, for its belief in one God conflicted with the official polytheism of the State. But its spread throughout the empire made it difficult for Rome to carry out the law effectively, and although the new religion was banned and its followers outlawed, persecution was sporadic. Sometimes it was local, sometimes regional, occasionally general; in all cases the Christian lived in danger of it. Thus Trajan (98-117) permitted governors to condemn only those Christians who were formally called to their attention by private individuals. To be a Christian was still a crime punishable by death, but the State would not hunt for the criminals, nor punish them if they denied the "crime." Other emperors, like Domitian in 95, showed no such restraint, and the danger of persecution was always contingent upon an imperial whim, popular animosity, or any incident.

Strangely enough, the first pardon granted for being a Christian was that accorded by Commodus, the one bad emperor of the second century, who ordered the release of those condemned to forced labor in the mines of Sardinia. Pope Victor I—during whose reign Latin be-

gan to replace Greek as the official language of the
Roman Church—was asked to give him the list of the
condemned, among whom was the future Pope Callistus.
The indulgence of Commodus eased the tension mo-
mentarily, but he did not abolish the laws against the
Christians.

Septimius Severus (193-211) departed from the lenient
policy of Trajan and revived active persecution by forbidding conversions. Maximinus the Thracian (235-238)
issued a special edict against the clergy, and as a result
Pope Pontian was sent to the mines of Sardinia, where
he died of ill-treatment. The first empire-wide persecution was that of Decius (249-251), whose edict ordered
every Christian and every person suspected of being a
Christian to perform some act of adhesion to pagan worship. He sought less to make martyrs than apostates by
torture or imprisonment. In fact he made both. One of
his first victims was Pope Fabian in 250.

When Valerian in 257 ordered Christians to sacrifice
to imperial gods and forbade visits to the Christian
cemeteries, Pope Sixtus II and also St. Cyprian, Bishop
of Carthage, were among those put to death. But when
Valerian was taken prisoner by the Persians at Edessa
in 259, his son Gallienus, who succeeded him, ordered
an end to the persecutions. He even restored confiscated
churches and cemeteries and granted bishops the right to
function as heads of their churches. This edict of 268,
the first imperial act of limited toleration, inaugurated
forty years of peace for the Church. Christians became
governors of provinces and high magistrates and were
dispensed from offering sacrifices. They were numerous
at the imperial court and in the army. New churches
were built to handle the growing Christian communities.
By the end of the third century it looked as though
Christianity would make a peaceful conquest of the empire.

But the worst was yet to come. Egged on by his imperial second-in-command, Galerius, the aging Diocletian
unleashed in 303 an eight-year-long war against Christians, their churches, and their sacred books. It was at
this time that the library and archives of the popes, like
those of many other churches, were destroyed. Every
Christian now had to sacrifice to the gods or suffer. The

death of Pope Marcellinus in 304 was followed by a four-year vacancy and considerable trouble in the church at Rome until the election of Milziadus in 311, after the persecution was over. The edict of 311, granting toleration to Christians, was a confession of failure on the part of Galerius. The decision, confirmed two years later at Milan by the Emperors Licinius and Constantine, ushered in a new era for Christianity. It was no longer illegal to be a Christian.

— 2 —

CAESAROPAPISM, 313-751

WITH the reign of Constantine (313-337), the first Christian emperor, the Church entered a new era. Though impoverished and weakened by the bloody and destructive persecution of Diocletian, it soon found itself endowed with churches, lands, privileges, exemptions, and revenues by Constantine. The Empress Fausta gave to the popes the Lateran palace which was to be the papal residence throughout the Middle Ages. But along with this generous aid in temporal things, Constantine inaugurated what became the constant policy of Byzantine emperors: caesaropapism. This means that the emperor considered himself the final authority in all matters regarding the Church—even to the definition of dogma. It was the new scourge and it handicapped the papacy during this whole period. In addition, the failure of the empire in the West, the barbarian invasions, and the extensive destruction and depopulation of Rome were other factors which limited the exercise of the papal authority and forced the popes to assume new burdens.

Constantine and Caesaropapism in the Fourth Century. The changes which occurred as a result of Con-

stantine's re-establishment of political unity in the empire
by conquest, and of religious unity through the Council
of Nicea (325), were not to be unmixed blessings. Constantine, though no doubt sincerely converted to Christianity, was not a theologian. He was too much of a
Roman to cast off the traditional attitude of emperors
towards religion, and since he had full power he did not
hesitate to try to settle religious questions. The Church,
on the other hand, seems to have been so elated with its
new freedom, imperial favors, and patronage that it did
not react against an imperial absolutism familiar to it
since its foundation. It did not realize at first that a
benevolent Catholic emperor could be as dangerous to
its rightful independence as a pagan one.

In the East, Arianism, condemned by the Council of
Nicea, should have withered as earlier heresies had
withered when condemned; but the Arians, bypassing
the popes, skillfully maneuvered Constantine into accepting them back into the Church and into giving them
important episcopal sees in the East. The heretics thus
established the precedent, which others would generally
follow in the succeeding centuries, of seeking justification
by appealing, not to the pope, but to ill-instructed emperors whose theology was adapted to political expediency. The son of Constantine, Constantius II, was, moreover, a determined Arian and considered it his duty not
only to define the faith but to cow the bishops into accepting his position. To a group of Western bishops who
challenged his right to impose Arianism on the Church
he replied: "My will is canon law; obey—or exile."

Despite their predominance in the fourth-century
Church, especially in the East, the Arians seem to have
realized that nothing could be permanent without the
approval of Rome. When the rugged Athanasius, Bishop
of Alexandria, refused to accept their heretical teaching,
the Arian bishops, after condemning him with imperial
backing in the Council of Tyre (335), asked Rome to
approve their decision. Pope Julius I (348-352) seized
the opportunity to break the long silence of the papacy
on the case of Athanasius, and at a council at Rome
which condemned the Arians he clearly affirmed the
right of the Roman see, as heir of Peter, to hear and
judge the appeal of Athanasius. Later, his successor Pope

Liberius was exiled by Constantius II for refusing to accept the Arian position.

Caesaropapism, which presented such a danger for the Church under Arian emperors, could be disastrous even under Catholic emperors. Theodosius the Great (379-395), who was as anxious to have Catholic unity in the Church as some of his predecessors had been to have a unity based on Arianism, undertook to make Catholic orthodoxy prevail in the strongly Arian East. Oriental bishops, accustomed by now to look to the emperor for guidance, did not hesitate, in large part, to reject Arianism by reaffirming their faith in the Nicene Creed at the Council of Constantinople (381). They also took the occasion to affirm that the Bishop of Constantinople should enjoy a primacy of honor after the Bishop of Rome, because Constantinople was the new Rome. Theodosius therefore broke with Arianism and asserted that the test of Catholicity must be acceptance of the "faith given to the Romans by the divine Apostle Peter."

But he still acted as a Roman emperor and did not hesitate to intervene in ecclesiastical affairs. It was Ambrose, Bishop of Milan, who boldly challenged this Western caesaropapism and made Theodosius recognize that the emperor was in the Church, not above it. The great Ambrose established a principle which was to have a tremendous future.

In the fourth century, during which the emperors brought the persecutions to an end, gave the Church its freedom, and even made Christianity the official state religion of the empire, the popes had played an insignificant role; yet their primacy in the West was widely recognized as the ultimate authority in the Church. As episcopal autonomy had long been accepted over wide areas, Rome usually acted only when appealed to. Although Ambrose of Milan was the most forceful bishop of his age (as St. Augustine of Hippo would be after him) men turned to Rome and not to such towering leaders for definitive answers on questions of principle.

The Fifth Century. The successors of Theodosius in the fifth century continued the policy of caesaropapism which had proved so destructive of unity in the Church and of the recognition due the papacy. Although the popes of the period rarely took the initiative in settling religious quarrels in the East, they did not hesitate to assert their position clearly when appealed to by eastern bishops. When Cyril, Bishop of Alexandria, appealed to Pope Celestine I (422-432) about the heresy of Nestorius, the pope condemned it, and at the Council of Ephesus (431), called by Theodosius II, the papal directives were followed.

Twenty years later the Eastern bishops gave their clearest collective confession of papal primacy at the Council of Chalcedon (451), the largest of the early Church councils. Here it was the legates of Leo I (440-461) who won an overwhelming recognition of papal primacy.

Such victories, however, were short-lived. The defeated heretics—the Nestorians after the Council of Ephesus, and the Monophysites after the Council of Chalcedon—fished effectively in the troublesome waters of caesaropapism in order to undo the peace established by the popes at these two great councils and to reopen the schism with Rome. Faced with the jealous spirit of the Eastern court prelates, the popes usually maintained an attitude of reserve.

The incompetence of all the emperors in the West facilitated the collapse of the empire and paved the way for the invasions. Odoacer, the chief barbarian general of the Roman armies, was to depose the last "emperor" in 476.

Even before this, technically the "end" of the Western Empire, the papacy, although plagued with disputes over papal elections and disorders in Italy under weak emperors, was looked to for leadership against the barbarians. It was Pope Leo I the Great (440-461) who went forth to meet Attila the Hun in 452 and dissuaded him from further invasions of Italy. A few years later (455) when the memorably named Vandals marched on Rome, Leo I was the only one who had the courage to face them and to prevail upon them not to burn the city nor to massacre the inhabitants. He could not prevent the pillage, however—they took even the metal roofing—nor the carrying away of captives to North Africa.

During these decades of trial the spiritual authority of the pope was at times supported by the emperors. (*See Document No. 4.*) But imperial policy was such that the popes had on occasion to defend their independence. One of the successors of Leo I, Pope Gelasius I (492-496) did not hesitate to assert papal primacy in language so clear that it has remained ever since one of the fundamental statements of Church-State relations. (*See Document No. 5.*)

The Sixth Century. Stability and peace returned for a while under the Arian Ostrogothic king, Theodoric (493-526), who arbitrated one contested papal election and intervened in others.

Then the reconquest of Italy by Justinian, in a long-drawn-out war (535-562) against Totila and the Goths, left Italy desolate and Rome reduced to a population of a few thousand. For the papacy it meant a return to imperial caesaropapism; popes must again be confirmed by Byzantine emperors instead of by barbarian kings. But no sooner was Justinian dead than from the North the Lombards poured into the exhausted peninsula and Italy was divided among Lombard dukes and Byzantine duchies, the latter subject to the emperor's official, the exarch of Ravenna. The Romans, lacking any effective Byzantine administration, turned to the popes for the defense of their city and the Duchy of Rome against the ever-menacing Lombards. Little wonder that Gregory I wished to escape after his election in 590! Yet he worked to defend Rome and the Byzantine provinces against Lombard encroachments and used the income of papal lands to feed and care for the countless poverty-ridden Romans. He also gave direction to the work of converting these half-pagan and half-Arian neighbors, and in spite of the crushing burdens that weighed on him in Italy, sent St. Augustine and forty Benedictine monks to England to undertake the conversion of that country.

The Seventh Century. The popes continued to be the great leaders in the defense of the emperor's territories in Italy because of the weakness and incompetence of the Byzantine officials. Despite the popes' loyalty to the emperors—for politically they were his subjects—the emperors continued their caesaropapist policy and intervened constantly in the affairs of the Church. In 653 the Emperor Constans II (642-668) ordered Pope Martin I (649-655) deposed, arrested, and sent to Constantinople for trial because he opposed the emperor's edict defining

the nature of the human and divine wills in Christ.
Martin, an old man bedridden with gout, was found
guilty in a farcical trial, was stripped of his papal vest-
ments in front of a jeering mob, and, half-naked, was
dragged through the streets of Constantinople bound in
chains. He died of starvation while in exile in Crimea.

Caesaropapism was such an essential part of imperial
policy that the papacy was to be freed from it only when
a Frankish king, Pepin, having conquered the Lombards,
founded the Papal States, making the popes independent
of Byzantine emperors and allies of the new Carolingian
dynasty. The Byzantine policy, the collapse of the empire
in the West, and the barbarian invasions had placed
crushing burdens on the popes of the period; but they
never thought of abandoning Rome when it lost its political importance and was reduced to ruin. Nor did they
fail to defend, even with their lives, their traditional
position as heirs of the authority of Peter. Of the three
powers in Italy during the sixth, seventh, and the first
half of the eighth century—Byzantine, Lombard, and
papal—only the papal power survived into the Carolingian period.

— 3 —

THE POPES AND THE BARBARIAN KINGDOMS, 751-1049

AFTER nearly three and a half centuries of Byzantine
caesaropapism, the papacy gained its freedom from the
Eastern emperors thanks to the intervention of the
Frankish kings. Within fifty years of the founding of the
Papal States, the pope crowned as emperor the great
Carolingian king, Charlemagne, who was to play a
dominant role in the Church. But by the end of the

ninth century the collapse of this new empire left the papacy without a protector, and it fell prey to the base intrigues of the Roman nobility. Never before nor since has the papacy been subject to such humiliation and shameful direction. Then, with the intervention of the German rulers of the Holy Roman Empire, things improved, although attempts at reform suffered setbacks and the Church would have to await the election of Leo IX in 1049 before witnessing the dawn of a new life.

The Franks and the Papacy. The eighth century saw the end of the old order and the beginning of a new orientation of papal policy. The hope of establishing a stable Christian empire under Byzantine rule was gone, and to prevent annexation by the Lombards the popes had to turn to the Franks.

Ever since the conversion of Clovis, king of the Franks (481-511), to Catholicism—making him the only Catholic king in the West—the papacy had looked with favor upon the rising Frankish power. The eighth century was one of intense missionary activity as English and Irish monks, after evangelizing their homelands, had turned to the conversion of Germany and the Lowlands. New dioceses and monasteries were founded by Willibrord and St. Boniface, and papal authority and influence guided this work and brought the new churches under the jurisdiction of Rome. But all this was possible only because of the protection given these missionaries by Pepin of Heristal and Charles Martel. The latter's son, Pepin, who was to become the first Carolingian king, continued this royal protection and encouraged the reform of the Church in Gaul, which had fallen to low estate as a result of the disorders under the late Merovingian rulers and of the secularization of Church property by Charles Martel. St. Boniface called councils in Gaul to restore ecclesiastical discipline in the Frankish Church and to provide for regular elections of bishops and abbots. His efforts were encouraged, and the decisions of the councils were confirmed by Pepin.

This close cooperation of the Frankish rulers and the Church induced the popes to turn from Constantinople and to look for protection to the Franks. The extension of Christianity in western Europe and the political order established by Charles Martel and Pepin prepared the

way for the establishment of a unitary Christendom—
one in which the prince was considered the secular arm
at the service of the Church in its work of Christianizing
the world.

The Founding of the Carolingian Dynasty. Pope
Zachary threw the prestige of the papacy against the
traditionalists and on the side of Pepin when the latter
sought to dethrone the incompetent Merovingian dynasty
and to found a new one. When Pepin was crowned king
in 751, he was consecrated at Soissons by the English
missionary bishop, Boniface, with papal approval. Three
years later, Pope Stephen II, failing to get help from his
normal protector, the Byzantine emperor, and rebuffed in
his efforts to persuade the Lombards to leave Rome in
peace, crossed the Alps to seek aid from Pepin. It was
the first time that any pope had undertaken such a
journey. Would he be received with the deference due to
the Vicar of Christ and the head of the Church, or as a
subject of the Byzantine emperor, or as a sovereign
independent of imperial control? Pepin received him with
a special ceremonial deference, and the protocol that
was adopted in advance was derived from the famous
document known as the Donation of Constantine which
Pepin's envoy to the pope, Fulrad, Abbot of St. Denis,
had been shown when he met the pope in the south of
France. This document, forged at Rome in 753 or earlier,
claimed that Constantine had given the Lateran Palace,
Rome, and the western provinces of the empire to the
pope. It recognized the pope as head of the Church and
as one for whom the emperor should act as squire. In
fact, as Stephen approached Ponthion, Pepin came forth
to meet him and walked alongside the pope, who was on
horseback, to indicate the deference due him. It was a
precedent which was to lead to a quarrelsome future.

While Pepin tried to avoid war with the Lombards
through diplomacy, Pope Stephen II consecrated Pepin,
the queen, and their sons at St. Denis in 754. The pope
also bestowed on him the title of *patricius* of the
Romans, whereby he seems to have recognized Pepin
and his descendants as protectors of Rome.

When finally diplomacy failed to induce Aistulf, king
of the Lombards, to leave Rome alone, Pepin led an
army over the Alps in 755 and forced him to capitulate.

No sooner had Pepin returned home than Aistulf broke
all his promises and laid siege to Rome. At the urgent
request of the pope, Pepin returned and again forced
Aistulf to submit. A Byzantine emissary was on the spot,
demanding the return to the emperor of the lands taken
by Aistulf; Pepin refused and instead gave the former
imperial lands to the pope and his successors, for he had
come down to Italy not, as he said, to please the Byzantine emperor, but for the "love of St. Peter." In this way
the Papal States came into being in June 756.

The papal approval of Pepin's assumption of the
crown, followed by his consecration, and the close collaboration of pope and king led to a confusion of the
spiritual and temporal powers. The Roman natural-law
origin of the State had become blurred and forgotten
and was replaced by the political Augustinism which
made the Catholic faith the basis of civilization. The
king thereby became the defender of the Church and its
ally in establishing a Christian society. The working out
of the confusion of the two powers in the ensuing
decades was to depend in fact more on events and the
strong or weak personalities of pope or emperor than on
clearly defined constitutional law.

Although the relationship between king and pope remained ill-defined, it seems clear that Pepin, by accepting
consecration for himself and his family, understood that
it was his duty to defend the papacy and to help the
Church: the clergy would preach, but the king would
maintain order, for he now had a religious function to
perform which he had not had before.

The new Papal States were in constant need of protection against the Lombards and even against the military aristocracy of the new state. When the Lombards
renewed their threat, Pepin's son and successor, Charlemagne, defeated them in 774, took the Lombard crown
for himself, confirmed the Donation of Pepin, and even
added new lands to the papal domain.

The Coronation of Charlemagne. Charlemagne was
more than a protector of papal independence. Zealous
for the welfare of the Church, its expansion, and its
discipline, he absorbed in fact many of the functions of
the papacy. It was the strong and zealous Christian attitude of the student of St. Augustine's *City of God*—not

any constitutional relationship—which prompted Charlemagne to dominate as he did.

To have the much-needed protection of the Franks
and to escape the caesaropapism of the Byzantine emperors was a great gain, but the new alliance was not
without its dangers and was to result in its turn in a
Carolingian caesaropapism.

In 787 at the Seventh General Council of the Church
held at Nicea, the Byzantine Empress Irene put an end
to the iconoclastic policy of her government. This council defined the Catholic teaching on the veneration of
images and recognized the primacy of the pope. But
Charlemagne at the Council of Frankfort in 794 rejected
the Nicene Council's position on images and requested
Pope Adrian to approve iconoclastic teaching. The pope
refused, of course, to undo the work of the Second
Council of Nicea, but the attitude of Charlemagne indicates clearly the caesaropapist character of the king.

When Adrian's successor, although unanimously
elected in 795, became the victim of charges by a strong
opposing faction in Rome, he turned to Charlemagne for
help. In a procession on the Feast of St. Mark 799 the
pope was seized and imprisoned. When friends managed
to arrange his escape, the pope fled to the court of
Charlemagne. The king, occupied with German affairs
at the time, had the pope escorted back to Rome and
provided for his safety there. To settle the controversy
which continued to rage in Rome, Charlemagne went to
the Eternal City in November 800. As the clergy re-
minded the king that the pope could not be judged by
any man, the affair was settled by having Leo III swear
an oath as to his innocence before an assembly presided
over by Charlemagne. The accusers were condemned as
rebels.

Two days later, on December 25, 800, while the king
knelt in prayer at St. Peter's, Leo III placed a crown on
his head, as those present proclaimed him *Imperator
Romanorum,* "Emperor of the Romans." This dramatic
scene—the great king kneeling before the pope and receiving the imperial crown from him—remained deeply
imbedded in the memory of men and suggested the
proper relationship between the two powers. Neither the
pope nor the emperor seems at the time, to have had, or

at least to have expressed, any idea as to what it all meant. Charles continued all during his reign to act as though he were the pope, and influential ecclesiastics, like Alcuin, agreed with him. For the son of Pepin the chief function of the pope was to pray; the emperor would run ecclesiastical affairs. (*See Document No. 6.*)

It was Charlemagne who intensified the confusion of the temporal and spiritual implied in the consecration of Pepin and of himself. He named bishops and abbots, called church councils, encouraged the education of the clergy, and disciplined it, all the while using ecclesiastics to help administer his empire. By confining the role of the pope to prayer he fused Church and State into a single governing body for all Christendom under his direction. For Charlemagne his religious function was the dominant one: the secular power would be at the service of the Church.

By Christianizing the State, Charlemagne had unwittingly laid the groundwork for the papal theocracy of later centuries. If the chief function of the prince is to protect the Church and to establish Christian justice and peace, failure to carry out these functions would entail ecclesiastical censure. Louis the Pious (814-840) recognized the logic of this when he accepted the public penance imposed upon him by the Frankish bishops for his failure to protect the peace. Logic—and the vicissitudes of history—would transfer the supremacy of Christendom from the emperors to the papacy.

The particular concept of the Church held by Charlemagne could hardly be accepted as normal by the papacy, however helpful he may have been in encouraging the work of the Church. The popes, indeed, sought to free themselves from the Carolingian domination shortly after the death of the emperor in 814. Both Stephen V (816-817) and Paschal (817-824) were elected pope without imperial interference. In fact Louis the Pious, son and successor of Charlemagne, recognized officially that papal elections should be free from any intervention. Although this was not always respected in subsequent decades, the weakness of Louis the Pious and the wars with his sons marked the beginning of the dislocation of the empire and of what was to become the ascendancy of the Church over the emperors.

Nicholas I, the Great (858-867)—the third of the only three popes to be called "the Great"—reacted strongly against Carolingian theocracy. This courageous and holy man, relying on tradition, reasserted the papal primacy of jurisdiction and refused to annul the marriage of Lothair II even when an imperial army appeared before Rome to force compliance.

The collapse of the Carolingian empire in the second half of the ninth century under the onslaughts of Northman, Magyar, and Saracen, together with endless divisions among the royal family, meant an end to the problem of papal independence versus Carolingian caesaropapism. It meant, too, that the popes would have to defend themselves and the Roman people would have to look to the popes for safety as they had in the time of Leo I and of Gregory the Great. Against the Saracen raids Pope Leo IV (847-855) erected such extensive fortifications that the area around the Vatican was called the Leonine City. He built a navy, organized an army, and accompanied them to Ostia, where the combined forces routed the Moslems and destroyed their fleet (849).

In spite of the turbulence of the century and the weakness of the papacy, people still realized that imperial coronation, to be valid, must be done by the pope. When John VIII (872-882) had to decide whether Charles the Bald or Louis the German should be emperor on the death of the childless Louis II, and crowned Charles, he did not acquire any protection—for he was subsequently murdered—but he did set a precedent for his successors of a later age in that it was recognized that the pope had the right to decide which of two claimants should receive the imperial crown. Yet the rise of feudal anarchy, the secularization of ecclesiastical property, and the usurpation of the elective power brought the papacy into one of the most humiliating periods of its history.

The Tenth Century. During the tenth century the papacy was debased as it has never been at any other period in the whole Christian era. Without even the semblance of imperial protection, papal elections fell into the hands of the infamous family of Theophylact. This ruler of Ravenna, his daughter Marozia, and her son Alberic, manipulated papal elections for sixty years

(904-964). Alberic's son was pope as John XII at the age of sixteen. His shameful life of debauchery and cruelty culminated, owing to his political incompetence, in his appeal to Otto I of Germany for help. In return, John XII crowned Otto emperor and promised to be loyal to him. From now on the German emperors would claim control of papal elections instead of the descendants of Theophylact.

The new emperors, busy trying to subdue the unruly nobility of Germany or defending their lands against Magyar and Slav, were not always able to intervene in every papal election. From 964 to 1049 there is a period of confusion and vying for control between German rulers and the Roman nobility. Among the men chosen, there were at times reformers like Benedict VII, a great scholar like Sylvester II—the first French pope and dissolute men like John XIX. Many were short-lived— murdered, poisoned, or victims of cynical maneuvering in a climate of decadence.

The need for a profound reform was obvious. During the turmoil of two centuries (ca. 850-1050) the clergy had become victims of the feudal disorders. Many were poorly formed for their clerical duties, many were grossly ignorant of canon law and of the obligations of clerical celibacy. Clerical marriage was widespread, simony common. Even worse was the extensive control of clerical appointments by feudal lords. The isolation of the clergy in an age characterized by little political unity, and the decadence of the papacy itself, reveal a grim and seemingly hopeless situation. Although the monastic reform of Cluny and the moral reform encouraged by a number of kings had done much, a successful reform could come only from the papacy. From the middle of the eleventh century on, the papacy supplied the needed leadership and inspired the religious movement which was at the basis of the great spiritual, intellectual, and cultural achievements of the twelfth and thirteenth centuries.

After the caesaropapism of the Late Roman Empire and the Byzantine period, the papacy had won its independence under the benevolent protection of Pepin. The well-intentioned though domineering years of Charlemagne gave way to the disgraceful meddling of the

Roman nobility and the intermittent intervention of the
German emperors. Neither assured independence nor a
line of high-minded men to the Holy See. To achieve its
aims the papacy, like the Church, would have to free itself from lay control. This was to be the work of the
Gregorian reform.

— 4 —

THE GREGORIAN REFORM,
1049-1198

WITH the pontificate of Leo IX (1049-1054) a reform
was inaugurated which was destined to rid the Church
of lay control and to usher in the great age of the medieval papacy—the twelfth and thirteenth centuries. The
ascendancy gained by the papacy coincided with and
helps explain the flowering of the medieval Church and
civilization. It took a long and bitter struggle to free the
popes, the bishops, and the abbots from lay control and
the abuses which plagued the Church. And once this was
over, an even more bitter struggle was to ensue with the
Holy Roman Empire to determine which of the two was
the ultimate power in Christendom.

During this period the papacy centralized control over
the Church, took the leadership in the crusading movement, and developed its canon law and the most efficient
administrative institutions of the age. But these great
achievements were marred by the schism of 1054 as a
result of which the Byzantine Church broke with Rome.
The tragic breach still continues.

Leo IX (1049-1054).   When Leo IX was named by
Henry III in 1049, the new pope insisted on having his
nomination confirmed by the Roman clergy before he
would accept consecration. It was the first sign of a new

papal independence. Leo spent his short reign traveling throughout Europe and convoking provincial councils at which he handed out stern punishments and made the local clergy conscious of papal determination to introduce reforms. As he made his way about Europe he attached to his suite outstanding men imbued with the same spirit and thus created a group at the papal court devoted to his ideas. In this way he unified and led the scattered efforts of reformers.

Nicholas II (1058-1061). Nicholas II took the next step in freeing the papacy when by a decree of 1059 he declared that henceforth the pope would be elected by the cardinal clergy of Rome. To assure the execution of this decree he made an alliance with the Normans, who in return for recognition as rulers of Southern Italy and Sicily promised to assure free papal elections. (*See Document No. 7.*)

The greatest figure in the papal reform was Gregory VII (1073-1085). This pope, a man of wide experience gained from travel and years of service as adviser to his predecessors, attacked the root of the evil which had blighted the Church: lay investiture.

Gregory VII and the Lay Investiture Controversy. In creating a new bishop three steps are necessary: (1) his election by the diocesan clergy, (2) his sacramental consecration, and (3) his investiture. By controlling elections, lay princes had been able to name their own creatures or relatives and even to sell bishoprics to the highest bidder. Consecration by the metropolitan bishop gave the new bishop his sacramental powers (power of order) whereby he could ordain priests, confirm the faithful, etc. Because this right of consecration by other bishops and the handing on of these powers was never questioned, there has been an uninterrupted transmission of these powers from apostolic times to our own, in spite of the widespread abuses of the tenth and eleventh centuries. The third step was the investiture of the consecrated bishop with a specific diocese. Lay investiture confused the granting, not of the sacramental powers of the bishop, but of the temporal assets (property, buildings, etc.) of the bishopric and the power of jurisdiction over the faithful in the diocese—a spiritual power. The lay prince used the ring and pastoral staff, symbols of the

bishop's spiritual jurisdiction, in investing the bishop.
Thus the lay lord was granting a spiritual power he had
no right to accord. Herein lay the abuse and source of
trouble.

The feudal princes had become so accustomed for
centuries to rely on bishops and abbots as officials of
government and advisers, it seemed quite normal for
them to choose and invest prelates with their office. If
the prince was virtuous and sought first the welfare of
the Church, he chose good men; if he was not, he chose
bad men and often sold the office to the highest bidder.
Many reformers wanted to eliminate such abuses as
simony, clerical marriage, and incontinence by reforming
the prince who would in turn, they thought, reform the
clergy. They accepted the system, which they justified by
referring to the religious character of the prince and the
temporal functions of the bishop as a ruler, but wanted
good men to operate it.

Gregory VII came to realize that it was the system itself which was basically wrong. The only solution was to
free the Church completely from control by the laity. He
inaugurated a Christian revolution against the idea of an
imperial state-church when he condemned lay investiture
and threatened to excommunicate and depose Henry IV
of Germany for practicing it. Henry retorted with his
Council at Worms (1076), which deposed Gregory VII
in insulting language. This was soon answered by Gregory's excommunicating and deposing Henry IV (1076).
Gregory did what no pope had done before: he deposed
the king, declaring he had lost all right to rule.

Gregory's principles were summed up in the *Dictatus
Papae*—a memorandum outlining papal powers. (*See
Document No. 8.*) The whole structure of medieval
Christendom was at stake. The king claimed that he
ruled by divine right and was responsible only to God,
unless he became heretical. Gregory claimed that as
Vicar of Christ he was responsible to God for the souls
of kings as well as of others. In other words, the king
was in the Church and as such subject to its moral law.
The pope could deprive the king of his office for failure
to observe the moral law, to assure a Christian peace
and Christian justice.

In trouble with his nobles at home, Henry made peace

at Canossa after doing penance for three days and three nights outside the castle gate. By going to Canossa, Henry recognized the rightness of the papal position, but soon forgot his sworn promises and forced Gregory into exile in Southern Italy, where he died. The king, meanwhile, had enthroned an antipope in Rome, who in turn servilely crowned Henry emperor (1084).

It was Urban II (1088-1099) who restored papal prestige. All the forces of reform, all who abhorred the absolutism and ruthlessness of Henry IV gathered around this former French monk. At the Council of Clermont, Urban II called for the First Crusade and found an unexpected wave of religious enthusiasm ready to sweep all Europe. He had won public opinion to his side and exalted papal leadership throughout the West.

Concordat of Worms (1122). The investiture controversy was finally settled at Worms, when King Henry V, the successor of the enemy of Gregory VII, recognized the right of the Church to elect and consecrate its bishops freely. The king would no longer use the ring and staff when "investing" a bishop, but only the scepter —the symbol of the temporal authority. The Concordat of Worms, the work of Callistus II, was a triumph of the principle for which Gregory VII had fought and died. (See Document No. 9.) To this great pope the Church owed its reform of clerical mores, its freedom to choose its officials, and the recognition of its ascendancy over the secular powers.

Callistus celebrated the victory of Worms by convoking the first general council of the Church in the West: the First Lateran Council (1123). Here the Concordat of Worms was approved and the question of clerical marriage settled: the marriages of men who had received holy orders were henceforward null and void.

Pope Alexander III and Frederick Barbarossa. The conflict between the independent papacy and the German kings was renewed thirty years later by Frederick I Barbarossa. This ambitious man, who sought to revive the old Roman idea of imperial power, initiated a conflict which lasted nearly a century (1159-1254). Emperor Frederick I challenged the papal position by reasserting at the Diet of Roncaglia (1158) the ancient pagan and Roman theory of imperial absolutism: the emperor's will is law. It was the old issue: Is the empire in the Church or the Church in the Empire? Is the emperor subject to the moral law or above it? Was the pope, as pope, a subject of the emperor or independent?

The pope at this time was Alexander III (1159-1181), the first of a great line of canon-lawyer popes. He soon found himself exiled from Rome and obliged to make an alliance with Lombard city-states who also preferred freedom to imperial control. The emperor, excommunicated, suffered a decisive defeat at Legnano (1176). The following year the proud Frederick knelt before Alexander outside St. Mark's church in Venice (1177) to ask absolution of the pope, who had preferred exile and war to sacrifice of the freedom of the Church and of principle.

The work of the Church had been disrupted by the nineteen years of conflict. To restore order and infuse the Church with a new spiritual life, Alexander III called another general council (1179). This council—which also met in the Lateran palace at Rome—proposed remedies for current abuses, and tried to prevent future schisms and elections of antipopes by a decree which said a papal election was valid only if the candidate received two thirds of the votes cast. (*See Document No. 10.*) The Council not only followed the path toward a strong centralized papacy, but worked to strengthen the bishops against lay interference and to assure peace and social reform.

The imperial defeat at Legnano (1176) and the reconciliation at Venice (1177) were soon forgotten, however, and papal independence was more seriously threatened than ever when Henry VI of Germany, the young son of Frederick Barbarossa, married the heiress of Southern Italy and Sicily in 1185. Dreaming of reviving the old Roman Empire by uniting Italy and his northern domains, and even of conquering Constantinople, young Henry VI seemed on the verge of triumph when he died suddenly in 1197. He left his three-year-old son to the care of his ninety-year-old enemy, Pope Celestine III— the only man he knew he could trust! The unexpected death of Henry VI changed the situation completely; and then, to succeed the aged Celestine who died shortly afterwards, the College of Cardinals elected the thirty-seven-year-old Innocent III, who as guardian of Henry's only heir was in a strong position as regards the quarreling nobility of Germany.

The "Two Swords" Theory. During the twelfth century the conflict between the papacy and the empire led to considerable speculation as to the relative positions of pope and emperor in Christendom. St. Bernard (1090-1153), a Cistercian monk and the most influential man of the first half of the century, formulated the "two swords" theory. According to this both the spiritual and the temporal powers belonged to the pope. The temporal power, however, was to be used by the prince but at the orders of the pope. The theory was the logical consequence of royal consecration, whereby the king became a quasi-religious figure in the Church. The king, therefore, was in the service of the universal Church with the function of establishing a Christian peace and so helping in the salvation of man. The canon-lawyer popes of the late twelfth and thirteenth centuries were to try to establish the legal basis for a Christian federation of nations, composed of the elements in a loosely organized, disorderly feudal society, under the unifying direction of the papacy. It was a theory justified by the political organization at the time and valid as long as there was such a united Christendom. The theory was applied to a specific historical situation and because of its contingent character never became a permanent part of the Church's teaching as to the manner in which the spiritual-temporal relationship should be expressed.[1]

[1] Pius IX pointed out the contingent character of the medieval temporal jurisdiction of the popes and showed how it had nothing to do with Papal infallibility:

"This right [to depose kings] has in fact—in exceptional circumstances—been exercised by the Popes; but it has nothing to do with Papal Infallibility. Its source was not the Infallibility, but the authority, of the Pope. The latter, according to the public law then in force and by the consent of the Christian nations, who recognized the Pope as the supreme Judge of Christendom, extended to judging, even in the temporal field, both Princes and States. Now the present situation is altogether different. Bad faith alone can confuse things and epochs so diverse. As though an infallible judgment in regard to a revealed Truth had any analogy with a right which the Popes, acting on the ex-

Schism of 1054. We have already noticed the strained relations which developed in earlier centuries between the Byzantine emperors and the patriarchs of Constantinople on the one hand, and the popes on the other. The Iconoclastic Controversy of the eighth century was followed in the ninth by renewed hostility resulting from the coronation of Charlemagne by Leo III. The decadence and barbarism which characterized the West from the late ninth to the middle of the eleventh century had widened the cultural differences between the East and the West. For during this period Byzantine culture continued to flourish. Relations between the papacy and the East were relatively insignificant.

Then in the eleventh century the attempts of the Byzantine emperors to regain their control of southern Italy and their subsequent expulsion by the Normans, with papal approval, embittered relations between Rome and the emperors at Constantinople. It was the aggressive anti-Roman Michael Cerularius, Patriarch of Constantinople at a time when the Byzantine court was degenerate, who led the quasi-independent Byzantine patriarchate into an open break or schism in 1054. Incompetence and lack of tact on both sides culminated in the excommunication of Cerularius and his followers on July 16, 1054. Greek contempt for the Latin West, unforgotten irritations, and profound misunderstanding engendered by the Crusades have prolonged the schism (except for two brief periods of reconciliation) down to our own day—one of the great tragedies of history.

pressed desire of the nations, have exercised when the public welfare so required!"——From an address to a delegation of the Accademia di Religione Cattolica, July 20, 1871. Quoted by Joseph Lecler, *The Two Sovereignties* (London, 1952) p. 63.

5

THE HEIGHT OF THE MEDIEVAL PAPACY, 1198-1303

IT WAS during the thirteenth century that the papacy exercised its greatest influence and sought to organize, under the direction of a line of outstanding pontiffs, a united Christian world on the basis of the contemporary feudal relationships and the one Church. Innocent III (1198-1216) came fairly close to attaining the goal. His successors continued to work towards it under increasingly difficult conditions. The longed-for unity was shattered in the early fourteenth century.

Innocent III. Innocent III was a vigorous young statesman-pope who devoted his life to reforming the Church, governing it efficiently, and exercising the direction of a united Christendom.

As a reformer he was in the line of Leo IX and of Gregory VII. The increasing bureaucracy which resulted from the centralization of ecclesiastical government in Rome, and the economic prosperity of the age, offered many temptations to the worldly-minded inside and outside the Church. To combat this, Innocent called the Fourth Lateran Council of 1215—the greatest and most fruitful of the medieval councils—for the purpose of inspiring and strengthening the reform element and of increasing the efficiency of the administration of the Church. With his tremendous energy he made papal power present everywhere to curb abuses.

To achieve a united Christendom in the light of the "two swords" theory popularized by St. Bernard, Innocent III needed diplomatic skill of the highest order. Men like King John Lackland of England, King Philip Augustus of France, and the Emperor Frederick II were not docile pupils when it came to submitting to the

theory. There was never any question of the pope usurping the legitimate functions of temporal rulers, but as
Vicar of Christ, supreme head of the Church, and final
judge on questions involving the moral law, Innocent
did not hesitate to claim the right to intervene in temporal matters *ratione peccati,* that is, by reason of the
moral law involved in political acts. (*See Document No.
11.*) The difficulty came less from the theory, which no
one yet denied, than from its application to specific cases.
Headstrong rulers resisted, and Innocent had to invoke
excommunications, interdicts, and even war to force compliance. On the whole Innocent III was quite successful.
Later popes like Innocent IV (1243-1254) and Boniface
VIII (1294-1303), defending the same theory—and
sometimes expressing it more forcefully—were to try to
apply it under constantly changing historical conditions.

Popes Gregory IX (1227-1241) and Innocent IV faced
a new Barbarossa in the learned and thoroughly unscrupulous Frederick II of Germany, who revived, with
armed force and a rare cynicism, the old quarrel which
had pitted Gregory VII against Henry IV, and Alexander
III against Frederick Barbarossa. The issue was basically
the same: was the emperor—in this instance an enemy of
religion—to re-establish a new caesaropapism by controlling the papacy, or would the papacy continue to exercise
its supremacy over the emperor and princes in the establishment of a Christian order?

Frederick II, ward of Innocent III and heir of the
kingdom of Sicily, had promised when elected by the
German princes in 1211 that he would never unite his
Sicilian and German kingdoms under one crown. But
the new king was much more at home in the cosmopoli-
tan culture of Sicily where he had been brought up than
in Germany. He dreamed of uniting Germany and Italy
into one empire. In order to maintain peace and win the
support of the restless German nobility he granted them
extensive exemptions and privileges. Then he shattered
the resistance of the Lombard League which formed to
oppose his invasion of northern Italy, and invaded the
Papal States. Forced to flee from Rome to France, Pope
Innocent IV excommunicated and deposed the emperor
while strongly asserting papal claims, but was unable to
organize an effective crusade against Frederick. Death,

which had saved the Papal States from the threat of Frederick's father, Henry VI, once again frustrated Hohenstaufen imperialism. The death of the excommunicated emperor in 1250 and of his son Conradin in 1254 assured Innocent IV of a great victory in his fight to defend the freedom of the Church.

Pope Boniface VIII and King Philip IV. The dramatic defeat of the papal cause resulted from the rivalry between Philip IV of France and Pope Boniface VIII. On the surface it was a quarrel over the king's right to tax the clergy, but fundamentally the issue was the same as in the conflict with the Hohenstaufen. That the result was different was due to the greater control which the king now had over the once loosely organized feudal state. The territorial gains of Philip Augustus and the centralization of administrative institutions and royal power during the thirteenth century were making the king so much more the master in his own kingdom that he could safely challenge papal authority.

There was increasing resentment on the king's part of papal taxation and of papal intervention *ratione peccati*, and a growing irritation at extensions of the jurisdiction of ecclesiastical courts. Then as a result of the new intense study of Roman law, a reconsideration of the whole "two swords" theory, which was essentially spiritual, took place. Kings began to doubt that they were only agents of the Church.

The dynamism of the new forces of unity around the king encouraged the idea of independence. Boniface VIII in the quarrel defended the traditional order established by Gregory VII and his successors. A canon lawyer himself, he had the law and tradition on his side and was determined to protect them. Philip IV was the defender of the sovereign state based on Roman law. He claimed the right to rule his kingdom without papal guidance. He distinguished between the king's independence as a public figure and his spiritual subjection to the Church as a private person. In 1298 the mediation of Boniface in a quarrel between Edward I of England and Philip IV was accepted only on condition that the pope act as a private person. Preferring peace to pride, Boniface complied.

By way of answer to a papal protest against the imprisonment of a French bishop, Philip IV falsified papal letters, aroused public opinion against the pontiff by vilifying him, and authorized the violent seizure of Boniface at Anagni (1303). The victory of Philip IV over Boniface marks the end of an age. The suddenness of it indicates the extent to which the medieval Christian order had been profoundly undermined. Political theorists of Roman Law (*legists*) subsequently tried to justify the event and to answer those who defended the papal cause.

The strongest argument of the legists was based on the truth that the state has a natural right to its powers and to the use of them. The disintegration of the State in the ninth and tenth centuries and its absorption by the Church in the name of Christian unity had for a long time obscured this truth in men's minds. The thirteenth-century recovery of royal power, which had been lost to feudal lords in the late Carolingian period, and the new interest in Roman law revived the knowledge of this natural right of the state. St. Thomas Aquinas (d. 1274) saw it clearly and so did the legists. The brutal manner in which Philip IV and his henchmen applied it did not make it easier for honest men to accept it.

The changing character of the medieval state did much to destroy the traditional concept of Christendom. The fourteenth century marked the breakdown of medieval unity and foreshadowed the emergence of the national state. The papacy did not surrender its supremacy over things spiritual, but it did have to recognize increasingly that the secular power had matured enough to enjoy its natural autonomy. The papacy would need to exercise its own spiritual supremacy in a different way.

The Papal Inquisition.   No study of the thirteenth century can overlook the Inquisition which has been the subject of so much controversy. It is an example of the close cooperation of the church and civil authority in order to maintain public order and religious unity. The papal Inquisition was a court, composed of specially delegated judges, to try and sentence heretics, who had become very numerous in southern France and northern Italy under the name of *Albigensians*.

Albigensianism was a complete system which rejected the Church, its hierarchy, and all the sacraments. It had its own strange ethics, its own social and political ideas.

Its extreme pessimism made it an antisocial force of great magnitude. It claimed, for example, that matter was the creation of the devil. Everything under the sun and moon was corruption and evil. Therefore, the object of life was to detach oneself from the things of this world and to free the soul which is a prisoner of the body. The most obvious way to separate the soul and body for these heretics was suicide, and there were many adepts who cut their veins and bled to death or took poison or let themselves die of starvation. Some did follow this counsel of Albigensian perfection, but it is difficult to believe that large numbers did so.

According to the Albigensians, chastity was obligatory; marriage and procreation were abominations, for they resulted in another soul being imprisoned in corruption, and to marry was considered evidence that one had abandoned heresy. Concubinage was frowned on, but was preferred to marriage because it was less likely to lead to the establishment of a family.

The heretics denied the right of the civil authority to judge them, since it was the creation of the devil, and denied the right of the Church to judge because only God Himself had that right. This "reasoning" could only lead to anarchy. The heretics were also pacifists, and oaths were forbidden—a revolutionary idea in a society based on vassalage and oaths of fidelity.

As the heresy was widespread, to permit it to continue was to invite social disintegration. This was clearly a case for authority to intervene.

Yet the Church was very tolerant for a long time. All during the eleventh and during the first half of the twelfth centuries, the Church tried to win over the heretics by preaching, argument, treatises, and spiritual sanctions like excommunication. There were many incidents in which the faithful, enraged by the conduct of the heretics, lynched them or put strong pressure on their rulers to liquidate them. Frequently the clergy had to intervene to save them from popular fury.

The civil power started the torture and burning of heretics in the eleventh and twelfth centuries—and resorted to this many times because they feared the clergy would be too lenient. In 1162 King Louis VII of France criticized Pope Alexander III for saying: "It is better to absolve the guilty than to attack, through excessive zeal, the innocent."

Toward the end of the twelfth century, as the heresy continued to spread, the papal position became firmer. At the Council of Verona in 1184, Pope Lucius III made bishops responsible for seeing to it that heretics were turned over to civil authorities for punishment. Obstinacy in heresy and cooperation with heretics were to be punished by temporal penalties. The temporal and spiritual powers had long disagreed as to the best way to meet the challenge, but by 1184 the two had merged their policies.

The efforts of the bishops to gain the upper hand were unavailing. Many of them were too ignorant, too worldly, or too indifferent; many had relatives who were heretics and they wished to spare them. Innocent III thought the condition of the clergy was largely responsible for the continued growth of Albigensianism and took strong measures to remove incompetent ecclesiastics. The preaching of the ascetic Cistercians and the new and zealous Dominicans failed, however, to dent the resistance. By the thirteenth century Christianity had lost its ascendancy over souls in southern France, and the supposed civil authority there, Count Raymond V of Toulouse, confessed he could not cope with the situation since so many of the leading nobles who would have to help him were heretics themselves. The disorder was abetted in many cases by men who, though not heretical, were strongly anticlerical or simply greedy and took advantage of the disorder to despoil the Church and to enrich themselves.

Finally, Innocent III called for a crusade to restore order and law. The crusade—which went on intermittently from 1208 to 1229—was wholeheartedly supported by the popes, with the intention of substituting faithful nobles for the many heretical ones. The conflict degenerated into a war of conquest to the advantage of the kings of France. It crushed the military power of the heretics, but not the heresy. The crusade had not solved the problem.

A few years after it was over, Pope Gregory IX established the Inquisition, a tribunal composed of inquisitors, devoted to reform, independent of territorial and family attachments in the area, and backed by the papacy. They were specially trained judges who carried out an efficient orderly procedure. The Inquisition was an itinerant court at which each inquisitor had two discreet and reliable local men as witnesses, besides a number of *jurisperiti* to advise the inquisitor on the culpability of the accused and to evaluate the disinterestedness and testimony of the secret witnesses. If the accused was found guilty, the inquisitor had to obtain the agreement of the local bishop to his proposed punishment, if it were to be a severe one. If the bishop and the inquisitor disagreed, the decision was referred to the pope.

In 1252 Innocent IV authorized the torture of heretics "without injury to their limbs or endangering their lives," as he put it, when the charges made were very grave and all other means of persuasion failed. Torture was applied by the civil authorities, but only with the approval of the bishop. Henry C. Lea, no defender of the Inquisition, admits that "references to torture are singularly few." [1] From 1254 on, the death penalty was permitted by Innocent IV and was approved by his successors.

It is clear, then, that the spiritual and temporal powers intervened firmly after many decades of toleration. The medieval mind did not recognize an unlimited freedom of worship when the result meant a complete disruption of the social order and constant political turmoil. Church and prince each felt they had a right to defend themselves when threatened. It was to be several centuries before men would realize that it was possible to have political unity amidst religious diversity. Heresy, therefore, was a crime in so far as it destroyed from within a city freely and constitutionally composed of Christians. It was considered treason to God, and therefore more grievous than treason to the state. In an age when the Church considered heresy as dangerous to the soul as a contagious disease was to the body, it is not surprising that it sought by strong measures to prevent the heretics from infecting the healthy.

[1] Henry C. Lea, *History of the Inquisition of the Middle Ages* (New York, 1888) I, 423.

6

THE DECLINE OF THE PAPACY, 1303-1447

The century following the defeat of Boniface VIII by Philip IV marked the decline of that driving spirit of reform which had inspired the Church since the eleventh century. Western Europe now became involved in the long, disruptive Hundred Years War and witnessed the breakdown of political feudalism and of that economic expansion which had produced the prosperity of the twelfth and thirteenth centuries. The papacy faced the problem of administering its vast organization with a diminishing income and was unable to cope satisfactorily with the problem. By moving to Avignon, where French influence was predominant, the papacy lost that supranational character it had earlier enjoyed, and consequently, lost great prestige. The so-called Great Western Schism (1378-1417) disrupted the life of the Church; nationalism and conciliarism were on the verge of triumph within it, until the election of Martin V (1417) restored unity. Efforts at reform, however, proved ineffective.

The victory of Philip IV was overwhelming. He pursued it relentlessly following the death of Boniface VIII by inisting on a papal pardon for his royal henchmen. Boniface must be disinterred, tried, and condemned as a heretic. The French Clement V (1305-1314), a sick man, was more interested in pacifying Philip than in reviving bygone claims, although he refused to countenance a post-mortem trial of his predecessor. His successors made no attempt to undo Anagni.

The Avignon Papacy. When prolonged disorders in Italy prevented the departure of Clement for Rome, he settled in Avignon in 1309. Since the popes were not able to return to the Eternal City until 1377, this period is called the Avignon papacy. Actually, the popes remained at Avignon chiefly because of insecurity in Rome and their desire to reconcile France and England, then at war with each other. That they were in any sense captives of the French kings is legend. What was unusual about the situation was the length of time they were away from Rome, not the fact that they did not live there. During the twelfth and thirteenth centuries the popes lived outside of Rome over half the time.

For many years the Avignon popes considered their stay only temporary as they worked, at great financial expense, to establish peace in Italy and in the duchy of Rome. It was only in 1348 that they bought the city of Avignon from the Count of Provence and built the papal palace there.

Clement V, weak towards Philip IV, assured a succession of French popes by creating a majority of French cardinals, who in turn kept electing French pontiffs. Of the 134 cardinals named by the seven Avignon popes, 113 were French. Clement V was generous to a fault. He willed away so much of the papal treasury that his successor, John XXII (1316-1334), had to resort to new taxes and a rigid collection of existing ones. A very effective administrator, his problem was not new. Already in the thirteenth century, papal finances were strained as a result of the centralization of administration in Rome and the cost of the wars with Frederick II and the Albigensians. Fixed land rents, in a period of gradual inflation, gave the Church less real income, and Innocent III had met the problem by imposing a five per cent tax on all ecclesiastical revenues.

As early as the reign of Clement V there was a strong tide of protest against papal taxes, and demands by the princes to acquire shares of them for themselves. It increased under the efficient financial administration of John XXII as new taxes were imposed to defray the cost of building the papal palace at Avignon and of trying to restore peace in Italy. Other factors tending to lower the prestige of the papacy in western Europe were the corruption of the cardinals and lesser officials at the papal court, where a host of petty rackets developed, and the conviction that the French popes were aiding the French kings against England during the Hundred Years War. Too many people thought of the papacy as an efficient tax- and fee-collecting agency dominated by an extravagant court. The extension of the power of papal appointment to all ecclesiastical benefices and the loose traffic in them—although it slowed down the trend toward the development of national churches by keeping the right of appointment out of royal hands—brought home to the grass roots of Christendom examples of abuses. The excommunication of ecclesiastics and princes for failure to pay taxes and fees to Avignon exasperated both laity and clergy.

While Clement V and Clement VI were too generous or extravagant and inclined to nepotism, the other Avignon popes were very economy-minded; all were morally above reproach. They were not, indeed, great popes like Gregory VII or Innocent III; they were, rather, overwhelmed by the magnitude of the problems facing them in an age of disruption which lacked spiritual fervor. The Black Death in the years 1346-1350 killed millions of people and spread despair.

The long quarrel between pope and emperor started anew with Pope John XXII and Louis of Bavaria, the claimant to the throne of the Holy Roman Empire. During this conflict the imperial cause was abetted by a great antipapal writer, Marsiglio of Padua, who wrote the *Defensor Pacis*. The struggle ended with the Golden Bull of Charles IV in 1356, which provided that the Holy Roman Emperor should be chosen by seven electors without any reference to the Holy See. The emperor, like the kings of France, would be independent of Rome.

The Western Schism. The growing criticism of the Avignon papacy and the fervent pleas of St. Catherine of Siena led Gregory XI to return to Rome in 1377. It was the first time—except for a two-year period under Urban V—a pope had been in Rome since 1303. On the death of Gregory XI the next year the Romans, anxious to make the return to Rome permanent, clamored for the election of an Italian who would in turn, they hoped, create a majority of Italians in the College of Cardinals. Urban VI, the archbishop of Bari, was elected in April 1378 and recognized as pope by all the cardinals for four months. But very soon he antagonized those about him by the violence of his language, his tactlessness, and his desire to reform the papal court without delay, while St. Catherine of Siena was urging patience and moderation. Soon a number of the cardinals declared his election null and elected a French cardinal as pope in September 1378. The new "pope," Clement VII, moved to Avignon with his supporters, while Urban VI, abandoned, named a new College of Cardinals.

Historians generally agree now that Urban VI was the validly elected pope. It was less clear in 1378. The schism[1] begun in that year lasted until 1447. Actually the circumstance of two claimants to the papal throne was not new, but never before nor since has such a situation lasted so long.

The Schism of 1378 divided the Christian world deeply. Each claimant had his own College of Cardinals, his own bishops, his own tax collectors. Each tried to find supporters; each excommunicated the other. Monastic communities and cathedral chapters were divided in allegiance; theologians and saints are found on each side. Such confusion weakened further the prestige of the papacy and offered excellent opportunities for nationalism and politics to assert themselves. France supported the French Clement VII, as did France's ally Scotland. England, fighting France in the Hundred Years War, supported Urban VI, as did of course most Italians. As nations chose sides, positions became entrenched, neither claimant would yield to the numerous pleas made to him, and on a pope's death his cardinals elected a successor; two lines were thus established. The despair caused by the confusion prompted many people to think that the end of the world would come in 1400, and they prepared for it by extensive preaching and extraordinary penances.

In 1384 the University of Paris, still the intellectual center of Europe, asked its faculty and alumni to express their views as to the proper solution. The most frequently expressed opinion was that both popes should abdicate together. Since neither would do this, a group of cardinals of the two claimants assembled at Pisa in

[1] Technically this was not a schism. A schismatic is one who does not accept the authority of the pope—the case in the Schism of 1054. In 1378 people did not deny the authority of the pope; they did not know which was the true one.

1409, but as the council had not been called by the pope it was not a valid one. Although it "deposed" both claimants and elected a third, Alexander V, neither "deposed" pope recognized the new "pope" nor the council. The schism continued therefore, with three men now instead of two asserting their right to the papal throne.

Germany at the time had three pretenders to the imperial throne. The winner here, Sigismund, managed to organize with the help of John XXIII, the successor to the Pisan pope, a frustrated and aroused Christendom to meet at Constance in 1414 to solve the problem. In view of the obstinacy of the three claimants, many serious-minded Christians came to the conclusion not only that a council was the only way of ending the schism, but that a general council of the Church had a greater power than the pope himself.

Conciliarism and the Council of Constance. The *conciliar theory,* as this position was called, was widely held and had many advocates in high places. It seemed to fit in with contemporary ideas about parliamentary government of states; the Church should follow the same development. It was encouraged by princes who hoped to influence Church policy through the ecclesiastical representatives of their lands.

The Council of Constance (1414-1418) attracted a great number of the clergy and of the laity from all over Christendom—some 100,000 people in all. To outwit the preponderant Italian influence, the English clergy, and then the clergies of the other countries, proposed that the council should vote by nations, not by persons. Thus organized, there were five: the English, French, German, Italian, and Spanish; each nation's clergy would have only one vote. Nationalism thus won an initial victory over the traditional universalism proper to the Church.

When John XXIII fled in disguise in order to prolong the schism, the council, to prevent a breakup, persuaded its members to agree that its decisions would be binding on the pope. This would make it the supreme authority in the Church and amounted to a denial of the traditional supremacy held by the successors of St. Peter. The decree held the council together after the flight of John

XXIII,[2] but was in fact illegal, as was the council itself since it had not been convoked by the true pope, Gregory XII, a successor of Urban VI.

The turning point came when Gregory XII, with the agreement of the members, convoked the council on July 4, 1415—thus making it a legitimate one; then in the name of peace and unity, he abdicated. By accepting Gregory's convocation the members of the council recognized his right to convoke it and also the fact that the prior decisions of the council were not valid and binding on the faithful.

After the abdication of Gregory XII the Council deposed Benedict XIII, the Avignon claimant. The way was now clear for the members to name a successor to the See of Peter, and Martin V was elected on November 11, 1417. The Christian world rejoiced at its newly found unity which ended the long schism. The papacy had won a victory over conciliarism, but hesitated to call other councils lest these revive it. (*See Document No. 12.*)

The wearying conflict between the papacy and conciliarists was revived later at the Council of Basel (1431-1449), but the interminable wrangling of this council and its failure to achieve unity discredited it. Conciliarism, from the beginning contrary to the constitution of the Church, could only result in failure. The pope who had to endure the machinations of the Council of Basel, Eugenius IV (1431-1437), gave the Church a sense of joy by bringing to an end the Schism of 1054 at the Council of Ferrara-Florence in 1439—but it proved to be a reconciliation lasting for only a few years.

The long schism had cost the papacy much prestige, and attempts to inaugurate a serious and much-needed reform at this time were checked by nationalism. The popes were to have to reconcile themselves with this trend in the Church by making conventions with the national clergies, and to recognize the growing independence of monarchies by making concordats with princes. Meanwhile the abuses which had engendered so much resentment continued. The snares of the Renaissance were already being set.

[2] John was caught and imprisoned on orders from Sigismund. After the schism was over he recognized the new pope Martin V.

7

THE PAPACY AND THE RENAISSANCE, 1447-1517

THE unity of the Church, restored at Constance, permitted the papacy to reassert once more its primacy of jurisdiction, but preoccupation with conciliarism and the need for restoring order in Rome and in the administration of the Church delayed the needed reforms demanded by so many throughout the Christian world.

Meanwhile the spirit of the Renaissance was making itself felt in the hierarchy and the papacy itself. The urban prosperity and political conditions of Italy had encouraged a new humanism, born of the love of the Greek and Latin classics. All over Italy the intense search for beauty and the flowering of all the arts, which diverted the minds of the elite from the medieval outlook, were often accompanied by the resurgence of paganism and individualism. Some of the Renaissance popes encouraged the new movement in a sane way; others did so to the neglect of their spiritual duties, and combined a love of art with political intrigue and personal immorality which scandalized Christendom.

Nicholas V (1447-1455). Nicholas V, the first of the Renaissance popes, brought to an end the Council of Basel which had plagued the reign of Eugene IV (1431-1447). The long absence of the popes during the Avignon papacy and the constant disorders in the Papal States had left Rome a city in need of peace, order, and restoration. Nicholas V was a humanist who wanted to make Rome once more the capital of the Christian world. The Jubilee of 1450 was an occasion for celebrating the newly won unity and for restoring the authority of the Holy See. Nicholas V wanted to rebuild St. Peter's (since the old church built by Constantine was in poor condition), to repair other churches of Rome, and to reinvigorate the religious life of the city. Founder of the Vatican library, he encouraged the search and transcription of manuscripts for it so that the new learning would have its sources at hand. Artists would cooperate and have many opportunities in the building program.

One of the great problems of the age was the threat of Moslem expansion in Europe. A need to save Christian Constantinople from the Turks prompted Nicholas V to try to organize a crusade and to bring the Byzantine Church once more into unity with Rome. The kings, more interested in their own national interests than in the larger issue of Christian Europe, frustrated these papal attempts, and the centuries-old anti-Latin bitterness of the Byzantines blocked reunion. Constantinople fell to the Turks in 1453; the farsighted Nicholas V, alone, could not save it. Successors like Callistus III (1455-1458), Pius II (1458-1464)—the last of the great medieval popes—and Paul II (1464-1471) realized the extent of the danger and also tried, in vain, to form a crusade. In their eyes this issue, together with the effort to preserve the independence of the Papal States from the encroachments of Italian princes, was the most important issue of the period. The efforts made to meet these two problems delayed, however, the reform of the Church.

Sixtus IV (1471-1484). With Sixtus IV the papacy came to a tragic turning point in its long history. A great humanist and patron of learning and of the fine arts, builder of the Vatican palace and the Sistine Chapel, Sixtus IV abandoned the policy of a crusade against the Turks and concentrated on strengthening the temporal power of the popes in Italy. To meet the intrigues of his political enemies, he adopted the cynical methods of secular princes and thereby lowered the moral prestige of the papacy. Neglecting the universal spiritual interests of the Church, he sought to impose political absolutism on the Papal States. In an age when distrust was the order of the day, Sixtus IV hoped to secure loyalty to his policies and to establish firm papal control of the Roman nobility by placing his relatives in key positions. Nepotism was not new, but Sixtus IV made it into a system of control. These relatives used their positions to plunder the wealth of the Church and scandalized the faithful by their bad lives. It was inevitable that those who profited under such a pope would try to perpetuate their power by selecting as a successor one of their creatures, and would oppose bitterly anyone who wanted to dispossess them. The popes of this period were like secular princes bent on achieving absolute political power and wealth while patronizing artists and scholars of the Renaissance. Under such circumstances the interests of the Church were bound to suffer greatly.

Innocent VIII (1484-1492), a weak man of base immorality, recognized his natural children and married them off in order to facilitate the aims of papal diplomacy. He and his successor Alexander VI (1492-1503) —the scandalous Rodrigo Borgia—were both elected simoniacally.

The latter, though charming, intelligent, and a capable administrator, was dissolute in the extreme. A man of the world, he reigned during the crucial years when Europe was stirred by the multiple opportunities offered by the discovery of the New World; Spain had completed her unification and become a great power, and France, having recovered from the Hundred Years War, undertook to invade Italy. Alexander's Renaissance predecessors had resorted to balance-of-power politics, playing one Italian prince off against another in order to remain free from them all. In the French invasion and the Franco-Spanish rivalry for the control of Italy, the threat that Alexander had to meet was one of great kingdoms, not of petty states.

It was Julius II (1503-1513) who had the qualifications to meet the worldly side of his problems. A vigorous leader, a daring general and man of action, he founded the famous Swiss guards (1506) to protect himself against the bandits of Rome and took personal charge of restoring order in the Papal States. Through diplomacy and war he checked the ambitions of France and Venice.

Although deeply involved in war and politics, Julius II found time to be a great patron of the arts. He began the construction of the present St. Peter's Basilica and made Rome the beautiful city it is through his patronage of the arts. He remains in history as a strong pope who exalted the temporal power of the papacy, often by means which shocked even the tolerant opinion of his age, but who neglected the work of spiritual reform.

The earlier scandals, however, had been checked.

His successor Leo X (1513-1521), the son of the Florentine Medici, Lorenzo the Magnificent, was a man of peace, highly cultured, the idol of the humanists. But he was a prodigal man who sought money by any and all means in order to satisfy his taste for luxury and his desire to build St. Peter's and other churches. Oppressive fiscal measures and extensive use of indulgences were resorted to for the purpose of financing construction of churches, hospitals, and public works. The artistic brilliance of the papal court was no compensation for the absence of spiritual reform and leadership. Leo's financial policies, as well as the long years of corruption in Rome, left a smoldering resentment to which he was indifferent. Secretive and double-dealing in political maneuvers, Leo was no match for the ambitious young Francis I of France, who undid the military victories of Julius II and forced Leo X to agree to the Concordat of Bologna (1516).

The Concordat of Bologna. By the Concordat of Bologna, Leo X recognized the right of the king of France to name bishops and abbots, and thus gave up the one real chance of exercising effective control over the French hierarchy for centuries. (*See Document No. 13.*)

The Concordat did, however, better the existing situation which had resulted from the Pragmatic Sanction of Bourges (1438). This royal act had accepted a number of decrees of the schismatic Council of Basel and was the fruit of French conciliarists and nationalists. Never recognized by the papacy, the Pragmatic Sanction purported to free the Church in France from papal taxation and to restore the principle of the election of bishops, but in fact led to the control of the Church in France by the Crown and to endless disorders in the appointment of the higher clergy and the assigment of benefices.

Leo X proved again how ineffective his diplomatic skill was at the time of the election of Emperor Charles V. This young heir to the New World possessions of Spain and to so much of Europe, would, if elected, be a great threat to papal independence and Medici power in Italy. All of Leo's efforts to prevent his election failed.

Two years later Leo died at the age of forty-six. His

sudden death caused a financial panic. His incredible extravagance and misguided generosity left the papacy bankrupt. He had created and sold offices, borrowed heavily from banks and friends, pawned papal jewelry and silverware. Even so, this had not brought in enough.

Under Julius II and Leo X the Renaissance reached its peak of splendor and magnificence in Rome. Much of what was built, carved, and painted still remains, a monument to the artistic patronage of these two popes. It was achieved, however, amidst a shocking venality and immorality, blind to criticism and the great need for reform, blind to the threatening dangers of heresy, nationalism, and individualism, blind to the greed and the methods of emerging capitalism.

By patronizing the arts the papacy gave the world some of its greatest masterpieces. But it failed to control the extremists and to cleanse the College of Cardinals and the papal court of evil schemers. It gave such an example of worldliness and corruption that it helped prepare the way for the great religious catastrophe which Luther's stormy genius let loose.

— 8 —

PROTESTANTISM AND THE CATHOLIC REFORMATION, 1517-1648

THE sixteenth century witnessed the revolution which destroyed the religious unity of Christendom. The revolt from Catholicism sparked by Luther (1483-1546) precipitated a series of religious wars which rocked Europe for well over a century. The Peace of Westphalia (1648) recognized and legalized the religious divisions as they existed after the Thirty Years War and rejected the right of the popes to influence the public law of Europe. Yet during this age of upheaval—political and economic as well as religious—the papacy reformed itself and recovered the prestige and moral leadership that it had gradually lost during the age of the Renaissance. The Council of Trent was a tremendous landmark in the work of Catholic rejuvenation.

Although the papacy had fallen victim to the spirit of the age and used the methods of contemporary Italian despots to maintain its independence, the cynicism and venality which characterized it for fifty years following the reign of Sixtus IV (1471-1484) do not reflect the state of Christendom outside of Italy. The general decline which characterized Europe in the fourteenth and fifteenth centuries had affected states as well as the Church. Yet amidst all the quarrels and disorders stemming from the Avignon papacy, the schism, the conciliar movement, and the widespread ignorance, there had remained a loyal attachment to the faith among many people of Europe. Many had clamored for reform, many had started local or regional movements to eliminate the accumulated abuses and spiritual sloth; the Christian humanists had sought to revitalize the intellectual and religious life of the Church. Kings, princes, and capitalists who tried to control it and grab its lands were as much in need of reform as the papacy and the clergy— and powerful enough to delay the reform needed. By the early sixteenth century, however, Catholic reformers, though numerous and active, had not done enough to head off the catastrophe.

Lutheranism. When Luther revolted (1517), Leo X, the luxury-loving Medici pope, misunderstood completely the nature and extent of the dissatisfaction within the Church and of the anti-Roman feeling in Germany. Luther's misguided courage and intelligence and his colorful, vulgar rhetoric quickly won him a wide following. His success can be explained by the inertia and indifference of the German hierarchy and by his appeal to German nationalism, which won him the support of Catholic princes. Emperor Charles V, who should have been an ally of the pope, was too much preoccupied with the Turkish menace and his widespread territorial possessions, and for the sake of peace was willing to compromise on doctrinal issues. In the name of "reform," Luther rejected the Church and handed over control of things spiritual and temporal to willing German princes, many of whom were more easily converted by the possession of confiscated Church property than any of Luther's theological arguments about "justification by faith." Thus he re-established caesaropapism and ensured the triumph of political absolutism. With a naive optimism he was to make the state the final authority as to what the moral law requires. Neither Leo X, who excommunicated Luther, nor the vacillating Clement VII could cope with Luther's triumph.

Large parts of Germany and all of the Scandinavian countries became Lutheran, as kings and princes, looting the Church of its property, determined the faith of their subjects. Calvin, in turn, established a church-state in Geneva and won triumphs in Holland and Scotland.

The Revolt in England. England, too, gradually joined the revolt under the headstrong Henry VIII. The Act of Supremacy (1534) whereby Parliament, usurping power, declared the king the supreme head on earth of the Church of England, severed the relations of the English Church with Rome, and united the spiritual and temporal powers in the Crown. Hatred for the papacy was popularized by orders to the clergy to preach eight sermons annually against the usurpations of the popes. Their names were removed from the liturgy, except for the invocation before high mass on Sunday: "From the tyranny of the Bishop of Rome and all his detestable enormities, Good Lord deliver us." The effect of fostering such a popular attitude, the confiscation of monasteries, and the foundation of a class with a vested interest in the new order, ensured resistance to a truly Catholic reformation.

The long reign of Queen Elizabeth (1558-1603), during which Protestantism was impressed on the country, undid the work of the brief period of restoration under Mary (1553-1558) and reduced the Catholics of England to a small minority. Pius V, informed that the English Catholics were torn between their desire to revolt against the queen and their duty to be loyal to one they considered a legitimate sovereign until proclaimed heretical, excommunicated Elizabeth, deprived her of her "pretended right to the kingdom," and absolved her subjects from further allegiance to her. The papal bull freed the consciences of those English Catholics who wished to bear arms against the queen, but also gave her and Cecil another excuse for making the lot of the Catholics worse than it already was. It was the last time a pope would excommunicate a sovereign in such a way as to free his subjects from every obligation of allegiance and obedience.

While the tide of revolt from the Church was sweeping over large areas of Europe, the papacy reformed itself, and with the help of many saints and great minds brought about a true reform—one which astounded Europe by its vitality. Beginning with the pontificate of Paul III (1534-1549) the Church was blessed with a succession of energetic and determined popes.

The vigorous measures inaugurated during the short reign of the Dutch Adrian VI (1521-1523)—the last non-Italian pope—were neglected by the weak Clement VII, whose quarrel with the Emperor Charles V led to the sack of Rome in 1527 and the end of the Renaissance in the Eternal City.

The Catholic Reformation.   Paul III, the first of the reform popes, ushered in the new age for the papacy by appointing outstanding men like Pole and Contarini to the College of Cardinals. For Paul the change must begin with the papacy, its court, and the Cardinals, and then be extended throughout the Church. The chastened College of Cardinals would ensure a succession of high-minded pontiffs to continue the movement. A report, *The Advice of the Commission of Cardinals on the Reform of the Church* (1537), drawn up on the orders of Paul III, bluntly and honestly listed the abuses and changes which should be made. It was the foundation for the work of the Council of Trent. The pope was determined, in spite of wars and of persistent opposition from the princes and many in the hierarchy, to call a general council in 1536. Luther and his followers, who had earlier appealed to a council, refused to come. After nine years of exasperating delay, thanks to the perseverance of Paul III the council met at Trent in 1545. It was to last, though often suspended by wars and politics, during the ensuing eighteen years, until 1563.

The Council of Trent marked the turning point in the Catholic Reformation. Dominated by the greatest minds of the age, it defined the Church's position on all the issues raised by Protestantism and passed a host of disciplinary decrees to eliminate the abuses which had so long encumbered the administration and poisoned the spiritual life of the Church.

Enormous obstacles, entrenched abuses, vested interests, political conniving worked against the reforms of Trent. The iron-willed, seventy-nine-year-old pope Paul IV (1555-1559) did not wait for the council to finish its work. A founder, with St. Cajetan of Thiene, of the new religious order of the Theatines which trained a zealous clergy, Paul IV ordered all bishops in Rome to return to their dioceses and to resign their extra benefices. A vigorous financial reform cut the papal revenue sharply. He put an end to nepotism and re-established that religious atmosphere in the Holy City which has ever since characterized it. His successor Pius IV (1559-1565) saw to the completion of the Council of Trent; St. Pius V (1566-1572) was to see that its decisions were carried out.

Definition and disciplinary decrees would not of themselves reform the Church. The papacy, which had given such extraordinary leadership by its own example and determination, found many throughout Christendom willing to help it. The new Society of Jesus, founded by the Spaniard Ignatius Loyola, became the spearhead of a drive to restore papal prestige, re-Christianize Catholic Europe, and win back those who had broken with Rome. Founders of colleges and seminaries, the Jesuits gave a new impetus to classical education; extraordinary missionaries, they revitalized the spiritual and intellectual life of Europe and carried the Gospel overseas to the New World and Asia. Other new religious orders, too, were founded: the Oratory of Divine Love, the Capuchins, Barnabites, Somaschi, the Ursulines, and reformed Carmelites also helped to take the offensive against Protestantism.

The popes modernized the machinery of papal government and gave direction to the movement. The Catechism of Trent, published in 1566, contains an authoritative body of Catholic teaching; a new edition of the Vulgate was undertaken and a new standard missal and Breviary were prepared. Pope Sixtus V enlarged the College of Cardinals to seventy in 1586—a figure which still stands. Two years later, fifteen permanent committees or *congregations* were established to handle more efficiently the spiritual and temporal affairs of the Church. The Catholic Reformation reawakened the latent or wavering faith of millions, and saved and recovered whole sections of Europe.

Pius V and the Battle of Lepanto (1571). Although preoccupied like his predecessors with the reform of the Church, Pius V played a decisive role in the defense of Christian Europe against Turkish domination. The aggression of the Turks in Europe during the sixteenth century not only meant that hundreds of thousands of Christians must live under Moslem domination, but facilitated the spread of Lutheranism by distracting the attention of the Emperor Charles V from dealing with it wholeheartedly. Pius V, seeing the Moslem danger in all its potential horror, succeeded in allaying, with patience and diplomacy, the bitter jealousies and suspicions of a number of Italian states and Spain long enough to organize an alliance. The combined naval forces of its members, including those of the Papal States, were entrusted to twenty-four-year-old Don John of Austria, the half brother of Philip II of Spain. Inspired by his deep religious fervor and his daring leadership, the combined fleets met the larger Turkish forces at the peak of their strength in the Gulf of Lepanto on October 7, 1571, and scored an overwhelming victory for the Christian coalition. The naval supremacy in the Mediterranean, won at Lepanto, was a tribute to papal foresight and diplomacy.

The Papacy and the Catholic Rulers. Despite the tremendous achievements of the reformed papacy and the Council of Trent, one major problem of the age was not touched: the reform of the Catholic rulers. The sixteenth century witnessed the transfer of control of the Church to the prince in Lutheran and Anglican countries. In Catholic lands a parallel assertion of absolutism had given the ruler an undue control of the clergy. In France, by the Concordat of Bologna (1516) as we saw earlier, the king had the right to name, within certain limitations hard to enforce, the bishops and abbots of the kingdom. In Spain and the Holy Roman Empire under Charles V, concern for the political interests of the emperor led to a similar subordination of the Church. The zealously Catholic Philip II of Spain (1556-1598) identified the interests of the Church and the papacy with his own—and they were not always the same. To attack the absolutism of the prince was to risk schism and war; not to challenge it risked making the papacy a tool of Spanish imperialism. France, torn by the religious wars with the Huguenots, could not be expected to view Spanish help against French Protestants as simply a matter of re-establishing unity of faith. A showdown with Spain was, however, averted; but the danger of identifying papal policy with absolutism was real, and the control of ecclesiastical appointments, exercised by Catholic princes bent on absolutism, hampered the work of reform.

The first half of the seventeenth century was dominated by the blood bath called the Thirty Years War (1618-1648). The compromise Peace of Augsburg (1555), which had established an uneasy peace between Catholics and Lutherans in Germany by recognizing the right of the prince to determine the religion of his subjects, denied any legal recognition to Calvinists. Often ignored in practice under the weak emperor Rudolph (1576-1612), the Peace became impractical with the spread of Calvinism. The election of the able and zealously Catholic Emperor Ferdinand II (1618-1637) led to the outbreak of the thirty-year conflict. The religious issue was soon lost sight of as the duel between France and the Habsburgs emerged, ending in the Treaty of Westphalia (1648) and the exhaustion of both sides.

The long war had crippled the work of reform, and the papacy itself lost the drive which had characterized it since the time of Paul III (1534-1549). Nepotism and a certain worldliness returned to Rome while the growth of nationalism and the bitterness of the war weakened considerably papal influence.

At the Peace of Westphalia the pope, Innocent X (1644-1655), was completely ignored. Church property was disposed of, bishoprics suppressed, and the usurpation of the spiritual authority established at Augsburg (1555) was reaffirmed. Religious truth was sacrificed to political expediency, and states rejected the traditional right of the Church to exercise its moral influence on the public affairs of Christendom. The absolute prince, Catholic or Protestant, would treat the Church in his territory as a tool of the State.

— 9 —

THE PAPACY AND ABSOLUTISM, 1648-1789

THE peacemakers in Westphalia rejected in advance the anticipated papal protest of Innocent X against the religious clauses of the treaty. By establishing equality among Christian denominations they encouraged secularization. Catholic teaching was ignored even to the incredible point of deciding that the see of Osnabrück, where the peacemakers often met, should be held alternately by Catholic and Protestant ecclesiastics!

From the Peace of Westphalia to the French Revolution papal influence, confined now to the Catholic countries, was sharply limited even here by the arrogant absolutism of Catholic rulers. The popes of this period, although themselves worthy men, were not for the most part men of great intellectual stature or strong character. In the Catholic countries the period is characterized by bitter quarrels over Jansenism, Gallicanism, and Josephism, the suppression of the Jesuits, and the growth of disbelief. The papacy had to meet the new errors in an age when strong Catholic rulers kept encroaching on the freedom of the Church. It is a delusion to believe that the Church or the papacy could be happy under such regimes.

Throughout the period France was the strongest political power on the continent and its cultural leader. The Catholic Reformation in France during the seventeenth century had produced such new religious societies as the Oratorians, Eudists, Sulpicians, and Sisters of Charity. There had been great saints like St. Francis of Sales and St. Vincent de Paul. But the movement, so full of promise, was blighted by Jansenism.

Jansenism. The growth of Calvinism in France and the Low Countries had led Catholic theologians to discuss the whole question of the relations of grace to freedom of the will. From it emerged an erroneous theory, condemned in the sixteenth century. A new impetus was given, however, to the error by the posthumous publication in 1640 of the *Augustinus,* a book written by Cornelius Jansen, Bishop of Ypres. It was not long before France was torn by controversy over an error which had already been settled by Rome. Strongly opposed by the Jesuits, the Jansenists calvinized Catholicism by emphasizing the idea of the chosen few with a sanctimonious holier-than-thou attitude.

Pope Urban VIII condemned the *Augustinus* in 1642, but by devious rationalizations and casuistry the Jansenists sought to evade the implications of this decision. In 1653 Innocent X condemned five propositions which summed up the Jansenist position. Subtle equivocations again explained away the condemnation. Finally, the acceptance by the bishops of a formula renouncing Jansenism produced the Peace of Clement IX (1669). The controversy quieted down for a generation, while the question of Gallican Liberties became the burning issue of the day.

Regalism. The danger to the freedom of the Church and the papacy of the absolute Catholic king can be seen in the conflict between Louis XIV (1643-1715) and the papacy. The Reformation had revived the caesaropapism of old by making the prince the head of the Church in his territory; the Church would be a department of the State. Under the old caesaropapism, be it that of a Byzantine emperor or of a Charlemagne, the ruler had a sense of his spiritual mission: the protection and propagation of Christianity. The new caesaropapism of the sixteenth and seventeenth centuries became laicized, and the prince, nourished on Jean Bodin's concept of indivisible sovereignty, claimed a complete control over the Church within his territory. This modern *regalism*, as it is called to distinguish it from caesaropapism, would subordinate the ecclesiastical jurisdiction to the monarch—absolute by divine right or not.

Gallicanism. Under Louis XIV, political Gallicanism, taking over Bodin's concept of sovereignty, sought to subject the exercise of the pope's spiritual powers to the royal will. The pope is a "foreigner," whose relations with the French clergy must be controlled by the State. The hierarchy, chosen by the king largely from a nobility subservient to the Crown, supported an ecclesiastical Gallicanism which would weaken papal control over the French clergy in favor of a national church dominated by the king. The Gallican spirit was already well entrenched when Louis XIV assumed personal power in 1661. Seeking to extend the right of regalia to all the dioceses and convents of the realm, in spite of the limitations imposed by the Concordat of Bologna (1516), Louis met the threat of papal excommunication by calling an extraordinary assembly of the French clergy in 1682. Under royal pressure the clergy approved a Declaration of Gallican Liberties—or more accurately, as Fénelon described them, "servitudes." These exempted the king from any control by the pope over the Church of France, proclaimed a general council of the Church superior to the pope, required that papal primacy be limited by the customs of the Gallican church, and subjected papal decrees on matters of faith to the consent of the whole Church. The king insisted that the Four Articles be taught in all seminaries. (*See Document No. 14.*)

Pope Innocent XI (1676-1689) answered the Declaration by refusing to invest as bishop any ecclesiastic who had participated in the assembly. As Louis XIV nominated for bishoprics only those who had attended the assembly, a deadlock ensued; and soon some thirty-five bishoprics in France were vacant for lack of agreement. Pope Alexander VIII (1689-1691) again condemned the Declaration. In 1693 the king finally gave in and the pope invested those ecclesiastics who had attended the assembly of 1682 if they repented their action. The papacy had stood its ground, but the Four Articles continued to express the sentiments of many Frenchmen, and by defining Gallicanism, helped to spread it to other countries where the doctrine was taught by nationalistic clergies and held by Catholic kings.

Revocation of the Edict of Nantes. It was in the midst of this quarrel over Gallicanism that Louis XIV revoked the Edict of Nantes. His zeal for Catholic unity, mixed with a strong dose of royal vanity, had led Louis to try to force the conversion of the Huguenots by quartering royal troops of questionable morals in Huguenot homes. Many were "converted" by these methods. In 1685 to impress the pope with his sense of orthodoxy the king revoked the Edict of Nantes. The pope, Innocent XI, was not impressed: he named cardinal the Bishop of Grenoble who had vigorously protested against the revocation.

Deism. Deism was one of the fruits of the Protestant Revolt. The denial of an objective religious authority reduced religious truth to a matter of personal opinion. Those who saw how illogical this was and who could not return to the authority of the traditional Church, gradually rejected revelation and the whole idea of a divinely founded Church. The Deists accepted only a natural religion without doctrine. Adopted by many of the intellectuals of the day, it became the fashion in the eighteenth century. The mocking pen and sharp wit of a Voltaire received more applause from willing readers in the so-called Age of Reason than reason itself. To deny was easier than to disprove. Arguments from the Bible and tradition were ineffective with those who had lost their faith.

Josephism. The case of Austria under Joseph II (1765-1790) illustrates the treatment of the Church under "enlightened" rulers. For this emperor the Church was simply a department of state subject to regulation even in minute details. The State would not only administer the wealth of the Church and supervise the formation of the clergy in an "enlightened" atmosphere, it prescribed even the number of candles to be lit during Mass. This suffocating atmosphere, in which the Church had to live, was characteristic of the age and explains why the papacy was in a poor position to meet the attacks of liberalism. It could not revitalize the clergy by naming bishops of its own choosing, for the absolute monarchs wanted docile men, not courageous and free spiritual leaders. How helpless it was may be seen again in the case of the Society of Jesus.

The Suppression of the Jesuits. The Jesuits, the great order of the Catholic Reformation of the sixteenth century, had been staunch defenders of papal supremacy and had remained such during the age of absolutism. Justly famous as missionaries and educators, they had become powerful and influential in the royal courts of Europe. Many of their members came from the aristocracy. Their success and wealth aroused an inevitable envy. Their opposition to Jansenism, which they worked to have condemned by Rome, and to Gallicanism, which would limit the power of the pope, had engendered many enemies within the Church. The Deists, however, by joining the opposition, gave the fight an anti-Catholic twist.

Their first victory came in Portugal, where the Marquis of Pombal, the corrupt minister of the weak king Joseph I, accused the Jesuits of supporting an attempted assassination of the king. Condemned without trial, they were expelled and their property confiscated; diplomatic relations with the Holy See were broken when the pope protested (1759).

In France a minor incident was built up into a national scandal. The enemies of the Jesuits—and they were many—were delighted when Louis XV signed the decree of suppression in 1764. The bishops and pope objected in vain. Clement XIII's famous protest in defense of the Jesuits was not even published in France. Three years later in Spain the Jesuits were ordered, through sealed letters to royal governors, to leave Spain immediately. Naples, Sicily, and Parma, satellites of Spain, followed suit.

Not satisfied with these "successes" and the confiscation of Jesuit property, the Catholic monarchs pressured the papacy into suppressing the order. After nearly five years of delay, Clement XIV finally yielded to royal threats for the sake of peace. The Deist king, Frederick II of Prussia, and the amoral Catherine the Great of Russia welcomed the Jesuits thus banished from Catholic lands, to show their contempt for papal bulls.

The victory over the Jesuits illustrates the unhappy fate of the Church and of the papacy in an age of absolute monarchs. Because so many countries had become Protestant, the pope felt obliged to rely on the Catholic monarchs to prevent further losses. This involved making concessions in order to prevent schisms within the Church or worse. The Catholic monarchs, however, in an age of absolutism, insisted on an ever tighter control over the Church in their respective countries. No doubt this insistence was due in part to their conviction that Catholicism was the true religion and in part to the contemporary Catholic—and Protestant—conviction that political unity depended upon the maintenance of religious unity; hence, the royal control over the Inquisition in Spain and the persecution of Protestants—and in Protestant countries, the persecution of Catholics and dissenters. It remains true, however, that the monarchs' excessive control of the Church not only identified it in the popular mind with absolutism, but stifled its spiritual vitality. By weakening the normal relationship of the papacy with the clergy and the faithful, the normal processes of the Church were perverted. In the conflict between the freedom of the Church and its security under absolute Catholic monarchs, the Church was forced into the false position of being identified with political absolutism. The French Revolution would put an end for a while to this enslavement of the Church.

— 10 —

THE PAPACY AND LIBERALISM, 1789-1878

THE French Revolution, which released so much pent-up fury against the Old Regime, turned viciously on the

Church. The papacy condemned the revolutionary excesses, and under the Directory and Napoleon two popes were seized and held prisoner in France. When finally the emperor was subdued and peace restored, the papacy was confronted with the problem of rebuilding a decimated clergy and an impoverished Church. Then it had to face the hostility of political and intellectual liberalism and a nationalism which would bring to an end the eleven-hundred-year-old Papal States. Conservative, tradition-minded popes were to defend vigorously the claims of the papacy and condemn the errors of the age, but by the end of this period, governments were hostile to it and persecuting the Church; many of the intellectual leaders and the industrial proletariat were lost to the faith. The age of materialism and of science was at hand; the papacy seemed to have lost the power to lead.

The French Revolution and the Church. The French Revolution started off with the enthusiastic support of many of the clergy who recognized the need of reform. These joined in the surrender of their privileges during the hectic night of August 4, 1789. The excitement of the moment and their Gallicanism prompted them to act, however, without consulting the Holy See. Then on November 2, 1789, the National Constituent Assembly in a desperate effort to solve the financial crisis, seized the property of the Church in return for a promise to defray the cost of worship, the salaries of the clergy, and the expense of helping the poor. The confiscation and nationalization of ecclesiastical wealth involved suppressing the religious orders so as to take and sell their property. After depriving the Church of its economic independence, the National Constituent Assembly then voted the Civil Constitution of the Clergy in July 1790. (*See Document No. 15.*) This provided for the election of bishops and pastors by popular vote, denied any papal influence in their choice, and reduced the number of bishoprics from 189 to 83. The Civil Constitution of the Clergy marked the high point of political Gallicanism. The Church, assigned its constitutional place in the new order, would be at the mercy of an "enlightened" State. When opposition to the Civil Constitution developed, the assembly required the clergy to swear an oath to accept it. (*See Document No. 16.*)

This split Catholic France in two and led to civil war.

Pius VI, poorly informed as to the exact nature of the attack on the Church, assumed that the king would not approve of the Civil Constitution until it had been submitted to the Holy See. But Louis XVI, under pressure, accepted both the Civil Constitution and the decree requiring the clergy to swear to accept it. The pope, fearing a schism, delayed condemning it until eight months after its promulgation. (*See Document No. 17.*) Then he suspended all members of the clergy who did not retract their oaths within forty days and refused to receive the new French ambassador (May 1791). In Paris an effigy of the "ogre of the Tiber" was burned at the Palais Royal and the papal city of Avignon was seized by the government. Amidst such passions all hope of compromise was gone. France was involved in religious and civil war within and foreign war without. The Age of Reason would have to wait a more propitious moment before settling the issue.

The Papacy and Napoleon. In 1798 Napoleon Bonaparte, victor in the Italian campaign, at the request of the Directory ordered an army to occupy Rome and to arrest the pope. The city and the Vatican were plundered. The sick, eighty-one-year-old Pius VI was taken to Valence in France, where he died (August 1799) still a prisoner. The papacy, it seemed to many, had come to the end of its long history. France was still hunting and deporting ecclesiastics, Rome and Italy were under the control of Napoleon. The cardinals had been arrested or had scattered, and the possibility of an election to name a successor seemed impossible. The "enlightened" seemed to have finally achieved one of their most cherished objectives—Pius VI was called "the last of the popes" by the wishful thinkers.

But Pius VI had foreseen the catastrophe which was to come, and prepared for the election of his successor. Wherever a majority of the cardinals could assemble, the senior member was to designate the place of the conclave and convoke the others. A majority of the forty-six members of the College of Cardinals were living in Venetia, which was at the time under the control of Austria, and the Emperor Francis II facilitated the practical organization of the conclave. Although the emperor thought he could direct the election, the cardinals nominated the man of their own choice, the Benedictine, Pius VII, on March 14, 1800. On his return to Rome he was given an enthusiastic welcome.

The ambitious Napoleon, as Consul, was wiser than the Directory which had sent him "to extinguish the flame of fanaticism." He saw that a France, bitterly divided by religious controversy, was a weak France; he would need a united one if he were to conquer Europe. He therefore made his peace with the papacy by the Concordat of 1801.

Concordat of 1801. Napoleon initiated the negotiations with Pius VII (1800-1823). In order to gain freedom for the Church to function in France, the pope gave up the Church's claims to all ecclesiastical property seized in 1790, in return for a promise that the bishops and pastors would receive an appropriate salary from the government. All the existing bishops would resign, new ones would be appointed by the First Consul and invested by Rome. Catholicism would no longer be the state religion of France, but simply "the religion of the vast majority of French citizens." (*See Document No. 18.*)

The Concordat was a compromise, one in which the papacy made great sacrifices in order to have worship restored and the sacraments made available to the faithful. By giving to the Consulate rights formerly held by the Crown, Pius VII, while enraging the royalists, made an initial reconciliation with the French Revolution. The prestige of the papacy and of the Church was greatly enhanced by the Concordat, since the forces of the Revolution, which had tried to destroy the Church, had to recognize the impossibility of establishing religious peace without coming to an understanding with the pope. It also dealt a serious blow to a Gallicanism, which had restricted papal jurisdiction, by recognizing the papal right to depose a whole episcopate. It was the first concordat of modern times with a lay state and served as a guide for some thirty others drawn up during the nineteenth century.

The Organic Articles. The enthusiasm engendered by the return to order and by the restoration of religious services agreed to by the Concordat was soon chilled by the unilateral publication of the Organic Articles, which Napoleon issued without consulting the pope. These revived the old Gallican claims over the Church in favor of the Consul.

By the Concordat Napoleon had sacrificed the principles of Gallicanism. By the Organic Articles he restored them; all papal acts and bulls, even decrees of general councils of the Church, must be submitted to the government for its approval. No papal official could function in France without the permission of the government. Bishops could not leave their dioceses or found seminaries without its authorization. A religious marriage could take place only after a civil one had been performed. The Gallican articles were to be taught in the seminaries. Pius VII protested in vain against this cynical duplicity of the First Consul (1802) which once more made the Church subservient to the State.

The Coronation of Napoleon. In May 1804 the First Consul had himself declared emperor, and in order to make his assumption of authority seem legitimate in the eyes of the French, as well as to reduce the opposition of royalists, he asked the pope to consecrate him in the cathedral of Notre Dame in Paris. Pius VII, fearful lest a refusal bring retaliation on the impoverished and highly controlled Church in France, acceded to the request in the hope of gaining some concessions. Well aware that the occasion was not a repetition of the coronation of Charlemagne, the pope did not, as agreed in advance, place the imperial crown on the head of the emperor. Although the concessions Napoleon made to the Church were limited, the visit of Pius VII to Paris served to increase greatly his prestige among the people of a country long infected with Gallicanism.

The vanity of the new emperor went to the point of imposing an imperial catechism (1806) which provided, among other things, for the celebration of the Feast of St. Napoleon—a saint nobody had ever heard of before —on August 15th.

As the emperor marched from victory to victory, he became more and more demanding. He insisted that the pope join his imperial system and support his anti-English policy. When Pius protested, Napoleon ordered the Papal States occupied and annexed as part of the

French Empire (June 10, 1809). Pius replied the same day by excommunicating the emperor and all those who had participated in the invasion. The papal bull of excommunication was posted publicly on the doors of the basilicas of Rome. When the pope refused to renounce his temporal sovereignty, he was arrested at two o'clock in the morning (July 6, 1809) and given half an hour to prepare his departure. Only his Secretary of State, Cardinal Pacca, was allowed to accompany him into exile. During the trip through northern Italy, over the Alps and into France to Savone, the ailing pope was greeted with reverence and sympathy by the people, who were horrified at the way he was being treated. At Savone he was subjected to an increasingly severe surveillance, not even being allowed paper, pen, or ink.

Since the pope was not free, he refused to invest new bishops to dioceses as these fell vacant. Napoleon would either have to leave them vacant or assign men who lacked powers to act. Without bishops there would be no peace in the Church.

After many futile efforts to make Pius VII yield, Napoleon in May 1812, a month before his departure for the Russian campaign, ordered the pope brought to Fontainebleau. Although deathly sick the pope was rushed to his new "prison" near Paris. On the emperor's return from the disaster in Russia, he renewed the pressure on the ailing pope. After six days of direct discussion with Napoleon, whom Pius liked in spite of everything, the pope, physically exhausted, signed an agreement which was "to serve as the basis of a definitive arrangement." It was clearly understood that the act would be kept secret. The agreement provided that the pope would invest bishops within six months. Napoleon, quickly forgetting his promise to keep the agreement a secret, published it as a concordat settling Church-State relations. Pius VII, so weak he could write only a few lines a day, protested to the Emperor against his new duplicity, and retracted what he said he had signed as a result of human frailty. Napoleon kept the letter secret and prevented anyone from seeing the pope.

After returning from the German campaign, Napoleon was to make a final settlement with the pontiff. But at Leipzig the emperor suffered another disastrous defeat.

Pius refused to discuss the question of Church-State relations further until he was free and at Rome. Napoleon had to yield and released him in January, 1814. The long ordeal of four and a half years was over.

With peace restored in 1815, the Church found itself impoverished. Its wealth had been seized and sold. The clergy had been decimated. Thousands of priests and religious had been killed or deported. With seminaries closed for years, there was no new young clergy to take over the empty parish churches.

The Restoration. In the name of legitimacy the prerevolutionary dynasties were restored to their thrones. The pope, thanks to the diplomatic skill of his Secretary of State, Cardinal Consalvi, recovered the Papal States at the Congress of Vienna (1815). Because of the seizure and imprisonment of Pius VI and of his own captivity, it was natural that Pius VII should look to the victorious monarchs for help in restoring the Church. To re-establish Catholic worship, the religious orders—the Jesuits were called back in 1814—seminaries and schools, the papacy, and the bishops generally, more mindful of tradition and immediate needs than of the changes wrought by the anti-Christian forces of the age, reverted to the prerevolutionary idea of an alliance of throne and altar. It was to be an uneasy alliance, however, for the kings again intended to control the acts of the Church with the help of aristocratic and Gallican bishops who were still predominant. The Romantic movement, with its nostalgia for things Catholic and medieval, seemed to justify such an alliance. But the Concert of Europe proved unable to defend the Vienna settlement against the protests of Liberals.

The Papacy and Liberalism. During the years 1815-1848 political liberalism, which opposed absolute monarchies in favor of constitutional parliamentary regimes based on varying degrees of popular sovereignty, was at work and led to a series of revolutions in 1830 and 1848.

The French revolution of 1830, in which anticlericalism was a useful adjunct in winning popular support for the bourgeois overthrow of the aristocracy, was strong evidence of what the wave of the future held in store. The Church would suffer from its alliance with conservative Catholic monarchs. Yet the anticlerical and anti-Catholic character of the Liberals, who opposed the Vienna settlement, tended to confirm the popes, mediocre personages, alas, in their conservative outlook. Revolutions in Belgium, Ireland, Poland, and Italy foreshadowed the growing strength of nineteenth-century nationalism— a force which the Concert of Europe chose to ignore or suppress.

A solution to the dilemma was proposed by the Abbé Lammenais, the leader of the Catholic Liberals in France. Seeing the danger of the alliance of the Church with absolutism and the handicaps of State control, he proposed the separation of Church and State, renunciation of the Concordat of 1801 and of the salaries paid to the clergy by the state. His anti-Gallicanism pleased Rome and the younger French clergy, but enraged the predominantly aristocratic and Gallican-minded hierarchy. With great foresight, Lammenais also attacked the ma terialistic character of economic liberalism which had placed the worker at the mercy of the bourgeois. When the French hierarchy condemned Lammenais's journal *L'Avenir,* he and his friends took their case to Rome. But they made the mistake of assuming the pope would accept their rash identification of their own solution with the Catholic faith itself, and so these "pilgrims of God and Liberty" met a cool reception in the Eternal City.

Pope Gregory XVI (1831-1846), without mentioning Lammenais by name, condemned liberalism in his inaugural encyclical, *Mirari vos* (1832). Basically, the modern liberties of the Liberals—freedom of worship, freedom of speech, and freedom of conscience—were condemned because they involved an interpretation of freedom based on a naturalistic concept of man. Liberalism made the human mind the norm of all truth and ignored the primacy of the supernatural. Lammenais, a brilliant rhetorician but not a deep thinker, had taken the theologically untenable position which made the common opinion of men the ultimate arbiter of truth. The Liberals believed that through freedom of speech and the vying of truth and error for men's minds, truth would win out in the end. The experience of over a hundred years does not seem to have proved the Liberal's contention.

Gregory XVI's condemnation of the ideals of *L'Avenir* was a matter of principle. In practice he was less adamant, as can be seen in the *de jure* recognition he gave the Belgian Constitution of 1831, the joint action of Catholics and Liberals, which had proclaimed the separation of Church and State.

The papacy's opposition to liberal nationalism came to the fore in the case of the Papal States themselves. One great obstacle to the legitimate objective of a united Italy, desired by many Italians, was the Papal States, extending from Rome to Ravenna. The pope had been the legal temporal ruler of this state for eleven centuries. But if it were surrendered to an Italian government, the pope would lose that temporal independence which was necessary as proof of his freedom as spiritual head of Catholics the world over; without it he would seem to be a subject of the shifting policies of the Italian government.

When the movement for administrative reforms in the Papal States became serious, and Italians began to agitate for the unification of Italy, Gregory XVI, conservative by nature and relying on the support of Austria, refused any changes. His death in 1846 prompted many to hope that the new pope would be inclined to make the overdue reforms.

Pius IX and the Roman Question. The election of Pius IX, who was not well known in Rome at the time, led to an initial optimism. A simple and kindly man, known for his love of the poor, his election was welcomed. More moderate and less antiliberal than his predecessors, hope for serious changes grew as a result of several of his first acts. His success in re-establishing a Latin patriarchate of Jerusalem (1847)—the first since the fifteenth century—and in reaching in the same year a limited concordat with Russia, providing for the appointment of bishops—there was only one very old Catholic bishop in Russia at the time—increased his prestige in the Catholic world. In 1848 the United States established a legation in Rome which was to last for twenty years. The popularity of Pius IX had encouraged many moderate Catholic liberals to hope that he would take the leadership of the movement to give Italy political unity and constitutional government—in a federation presided over by the pope.

While Pius IX favored weakening Austrian influence in Italy and sought to achieve this by drawing different Italian states closer together in a customs union and defensive league, he could not seriously consider the idea of leading or declaring a war on Catholic Austria. When this became clear, opinion in Italy grew hostile and direction of the movement for unification was taken over by radical elements. The situation soon got out of hand in Rome itself, and the pope left it in November 1848 for Gaeta, where he planned to board a French ship for France. The Roman Republic, proclaimed in February 1849, declared the temporal power of the popes at an end. Persuaded not to go to France, the pope appealed to Austria, France, Spain, and Naples to intervene militarily. Louis Napoleon, president of France, sent a French force which occupied Rome while Austrian troops also occupied parts of the Papal States. The pope returned to Rome in April 1850, where his independence was to be guaranteed by a French force until 1870.

The restoration of papal authority in the Papal States in 1849, with the support of foreign troops, meant a return to political conservatism. Pius IX made a number of administrative and economic reforms, which along with a general recovery led to a period of relative peace. But key positions in the temporal administration of the Papal States were still in the hands of ecclesiastics lacking initiative and energy, and the desire of the bourgeoisie for more political freedom made the conservative government of Pius IX the subject of criticism when compared to the more prosperous and constitutional government of the kingdom of Sardinia-Piedmont.

Cavour, prime minister of the kingdom of Sardinia-Piedmont, cleverly exploited the existing discontent in the Papal States while urging the unification of Italy around the House of Savoy. From 1848 on, the problem of the Papal States had become a political rather than an economic one. As long as Pius IX and his advisers considered the idea of a united and free Italy to be incompatible with the sovereign independence of the pope, the papacy faced an insoluble dilemma; and as long as Sardinia-Piedmont followed an antiecclesiastical policy, the papacy could hardly encourage Cavour's plans for unification. Pius IX, aware of his inability to meet difficult political situations, had entrusted temporal affairs to his Secretary of State, Cardinal Antonelli. This pro-Austrian old-regime type of cardinal followed, with great cleverness, a delaying action in order to postpone the inevitable loss of the Papal States.

When Cavour and Louis Napoleon, now emperor, carried out their carefully planned expulsion of the Austrians from northern Italy in 1859, the movement for unification got out of hand. Although Napoleon III refused to recognize the extension of the kingdom of Sardinia-Piedmont into central Italy, he did nothing to prevent it. When King Victor Emmanuel urged the pope to recognize the loss of Romagna, Pius IX refused. He could not, he said, surrender territory which he held in trust for all Catholics, to a government famous for its secularization of Church property, however sincere may have been the good intentions of Cavour. The death of Cavour was followed by negotiations between the Vatican and the House of Savoy, but these were made difficult by the increasingly anticlerical character of Italian politicians. However, Catholic opinion in France and the presence of French troops delayed the incorporation of the city of Rome into the kingdom of Italy until 1870.

With the seizure of Rome, the Italian government, anxious to reassure Catholic powers of its good intentions, voted the Law of Papal Guaranties which determined the position of the pope and the relations of Church and State in Italy. The law assured the pope of his independence and liberty. Pius IX rejected it completely, as well as the indemnities promised, because the law lacked international guaranties and did not recognize the sovereign character of the pope. The revokable promise of a state for which only too often honor had been opportunism could hardly be considered sufficient protection. Pius IX considered himself therefore a "prisoner in the Vatican"—as did his successors until 1929. Although the government and kings in the years following the seizure of Rome sought at times to improve relations with the papacy, the left-wing politicians and Freemasons, who had been actively hostile since 1859, obliged the government to follow a hateful policy: confiscation of most of the convents in Rome, slanders in the press, prohibition of religious processions and pilgrimages, etc.

Quanta Cura and the Syllabus of Errors. Before the question of the Papal States had reached the "solution" of 1870, Pius IX issued in 1864 the encyclical *Quanta cura*—a landmark in nineteenth-century history. The excesses of the revolutions of 1848, the increasing hostility of Liberals to the Church, the influence of liberalism on religious ideas, and the identification of social progress with the secularist and rationalist state, prompted him to launch an attack on current errors. In this letter Pius IX condemned rationalism, Gallicanism, socialism, naturalism, separation of Church and State, and the modern liberties. Appended to the encyclical was a *Syllabus of Errors* containing eighty propositions extracted from various papal documents, which had already condemned these errors. Isolated from their original context some of the propositions lent themselves to a meaning which was neither intended nor contained in the original context. The loosely worded last proposition, for example, which implied that the pope was against progress and modern civilization was, in its original context, aimed at those who would deny the Church any influence whatever in modern society. The *Syllabus*, like other historical documents, has to be considered in the light of the period in which it was issued.

At the time of its publication the *Syllabus* caused an uproar which disheartened Catholic Liberals and delighted those hostile to the Church. The condemnation of freedom of worship, freedom of conscience, and freedom of speech was issued because the Liberals, who advocated them, justified them from a rationalistic point of view, which made man the final judge of religious reality and denied that God had ever revealed anything definite which men must respect. What Liberals too often meant by freedom of conscience was freedom from conscience. The idea that one religion was as good as another was another example of the liberal error of making the natural powers of the human mind the ultimate judge of religious reality, and of denying that the Divine Christ had founded the only true Church. The pope condemned, therefore, this liberal indifferentism, though he recognized that in practice the position of those who disagreed must be respected.

The Vatican Council (1870). The growing hostility of governments to the papacy, and the seizure of papal territories by the Sardinian monarchy, seemed to indicate that the pope would soon be cut off from the possibility of meeting with his bishops. Wishing to complete the attack on rationalism and to consult with the bishops on the Church-State problem, he called a general council of the Church to define explicitly the traditional teaching concerning the primacy of Rome. This council, the first since the Council of Trent (1543-1563), was called in June 1867; it met in December 1869 and recessed for the summer, its work unfinished, in July 1870. But the seizure of Rome by the Italian government, after Napoleon III withdrew the French troops there at the outbreak of the Franco-Prussian War, prompted Pius IX, who felt that the Council would no longer be free, to adjourn the fall session *sine die*.

Its most spectacular achievement, because of the controversy it caused and the publicity it received, was the proclamation of the dogma of papal infallibility—a question raised after the council had assembled and on the initiative of a group of bishops. Even more important, however, was the decree on the primacy of the pope and that which defines that man can know God through his natural reason. (*See Document No. 19.*) In an age of rationalism the Church had to defend the powers of reason.

The proclamation of papal infallibility was an excuse in Germany for the *Kulturkampf* of Bismarck. This persecution of the Church troubled the last years of the reign of Pius IX. In France the Third Republic became increasingly anticlerical and anti-Christian, Austria denounced its Concordat of 1855, while Switzerland and Spain adopted hostile measures. The Church and the papacy seemed to be losing ground everywhere.

The death of Pius IX in 1878 at the age of eighty-five brought to an end the longest reign in the history of the papacy since that of St. Peter. He had dealt a deathblow to ecclesiastical Gallicanism by the Vatican Council decree on the primacy of the pope, as the clergy and the faithful rallied to the pope for support. He had centralized the power of the papacy over the Church as had never been the case before, and gave great impetus to missionary activity all over the world. He re-established hierarchies in England, Scotland, and Holland for the first time since the Reformation and did not hesitate to condemn the fashionable intellectual errors of his age. But at the same time he did not see the importance of the economic and social issues raised by the awakening of social consciousness and the increasing number of exploited workers, nor the need for restating the policies of the Church and its outlook in the light of the new order which had emerged during the century. This would be the work of his successor.

— 11 —

THE PAPACY IN THE CONTEMPORARY WORLD, 1878 1956

THE pontificate of Leo XIII (1878-1903) inaugurated a new age in the history of the papacy. The new pope was a man wonderfully farsighted, gifted with practical wisdom and patience, and one who saw things as they are. With him the papacy would take a new approach to its historic mission of Christianizing the world. Like his successors, he recognized that the great changes which had occurred since the French Revolution were permanent, and was determined to live with the new order created by the Industrial Revolution and victorious liberalism.

All the popes of this period have stood firm against persecution and in numerous papal encyclicals have analyzed the errors of their times and set out the reme-

dies for them with a clarity and wisdom never so richly
or so profusely given to the faithful in the whole history
of the Church. In 1929 the question of papal independence vis-à-vis Italy was finally settled. By their unstinting
works of charity during the two World Wars, their firmness in resisting the challenge of totalitarian states of the
twentieth century, and their efforts to win men to the
ways of peace, these five popes have won the respect of
men of all faiths and of those with none.

Leo XIII. The election of the Bishop of Perugia in
1878 brought to the papal throne the Church's greatest
pope since the Catholic Reformation. This man of frail
health and strong mind had to face the challenge of an
Italy governed by unscrupulous men full of hatred for
the Church. The Germany of Bismarck was still persecuting it, with the traditional smugness of those who believe that might makes right, and soon the France of the
Third Republic would show how antireligious its government could be. With Germany, Leo XIII won, in France
he failed for the most part, while in Italy nothing could
even be attempted.

Leo XIII and Germany. Bismarck's triumphs, culminating in the establishment of the German Empire in
1871, were not universally approved in Germany. The
Catholic states of southern Germany had no enthusiasm
for a unification and concentration of power in the hands
of the militaristic and Lutheran Junkers of Prussia; they
defended states rights in order to escape the heavy hand
of Bismarck. To overcome their opposition Bismarck
launched a concentrated attack on the Catholic Church
in Germany. As he would get more support for an attack
on the Church than for one on states rights, he began
the *Kulturkampf*—the so-called battle for civilization—
by expelling the Jesuits in 1872. In the next two years
the May laws required that every bishop and priest in
Germany be a German citizen, a graduate of a German
state university, and approved by the State. German
seminaries were subjected to state supervision, and Polish
Catholics living in Germany must be given religious
instruction in German.

The Church could accept neither this appeal to nationalism nor this subjection to the State. German
Catholics refused to obey the laws; bishops and priests

were therefore jailed or exiled. German Catholics, organized in the Catholic Center Party, won wide support for their program of religious liberty and social reforms, and Leo XIII gave them constant encouragement. Bismarck, surprised by the fervor of the Catholic resistance, became alarmed at the growth of socialism in Germany. Facing the opposition of the Socialists and Center Party in Parliament, he sought by making a few concessions to establish a *modus vivendi* without abrogating the May laws. Leo XIII with firmness insisted that the unjust laws be dropped *in toto* and with great diplomatic skill avoided the subtle traps of the aging chancellor. In 1882 diplomatic relations with the Vatican, broken off in 1872, were resumed, and in the following years the worst anti-Catholic measures were repealed. The political needs of Germany, the heroic resistance of the German Catholics, the skill and firmness of Leo XIII had produced what was to be his greatest diplomatic achievement.

Leo XIII and France. Following the defeat of the Franco-Prussian War and the overthrow of the empire of Louis Napoleon, France established the Third Republic in 1875. This new government became bitterly hostile to the Church and taxed all the ingenuity and patience Leo XIII could muster. The most important Catholic laymen and ecclesiastics at the time were royalists opposed to the Republic, and French Catholics generally were themselves strongly divided as to how to meet the antireligious action of the government. Accusing the Catholics of disloyalty, the anticlerical Republicans passed bills denying religious communities the right to teach without authorization from the government and prohibited religious instruction in the new system of free public schools. The Jesuits, whose suppression had been lifted in 1814, were again expelled from France. Marriage, to be legal, had to be performed by civil authorities, and civil courts could grant divorces. These early "laic laws" were supposed to strengthen the Republic and to curb Catholic influence. When the religious congregations were expelled in 1880, Leo XIII protested energetically but in vain. However, he sought to diminish the tension and to show his good will. In 1890 Archbishop Lavigerie of Algiers at a luncheon in honor of the officers of a French naval force which had landed at Algiers made an appeal for the union of all Frenchmen around the Republic. The archbishop, who spoke the thoughts of Leo XIII, and the pope himself were flooded with protests from enraged monarchists. By way of reply Leo XIII made Lavigerie a cardinal. To make perfectly clear his position, the pope addressed an encyclical to the French bishops and Catholics in which he appealed to them to give up their monarchist dreams, to accept the Republic, and to seek justice for the Church within the framework of the Republican constitution. But in vain, for the majority of French Catholics refused to follow the wise advice of the pope. The republican leaders of France, who had called the Catholics disloyal for their defense of monarchy, showed their true colors when they scorned those Catholics who did rally to the Republic. At heart their hatred of the Church was greater than their love of the Republic. Leo XIII had made a courageous attempt to dissociate the Church from any alliance with monarchy, but his attempt in France was seemingly a failure during his own lifetime.

Leo XIII and Italy. The hostility of the Italian government toward Leo XIII was as strong as it had been toward Pius IX. The hatred of political leaders for the Church and especially for the papacy continued unabated. Even Leo XIII with all his skill could do little but protest against the vilification and abuse, the constant interference in ecclesiastical affairs. In spite of the Law of Papal Guaranties whereby the pope was free to name bishops for the Church in Italy, the government, during vacancies, depleted the resources of bishoprics and delayed for months or years the right of new bishops to occupy their sees.

In July 1881 the remains of Pius IX were transferred from St. Peter's to the Church of San Lorenzo. Although the government had approved the transfer, which took place at midnight, the procession was attacked by a mob which almost succeeded in throwing the coffin into the Tiber. The government cynically managed not to prevent this scandalous outrage. Such incidents prompted Leo XIII to consider seriously leaving Rome to take up residence outside of Italy. The insults and abuse of the antireligious government had won wide sympathy for the pontiff abroad. In the atmosphere created by the suppression of religious communities, the seizure of ecclesiastical property, and the suppression of the Catholic press, the Roman question could not be solved. Leo XIII, like Pius IX, had to live his whole pontificate as a "prisoner of the Vatican."

Although he failed in France and Italy, Leo XIII reached the outside world through a series of encyclicals which rank among the greatest monuments of the contemporary period—a corpus of Christian wisdom. In them he manifested his vision by showing how the Church could live in the modern world.

Leo XIII's Encyclicals. Leo XIII has been the greatest teacher of the contemporary Church. He laid the basis for his whole program of reconstructing a Christian order in *Aeterni patris* (1879) in which he called for a restoration of the teaching of St. Thomas Aquinas in colleges and universities. St. Thomas would set Catholics to study their religion first of all for its own sake. His philosophic mind would be the corrective for the narrow-mindedness of liberalism which denied the existence of God, of a supernatural order, and of man's duty to submit to it. To encourage learning, Leo opened the Vatican archives to the scholars of the world, encouraged the study of history among Catholics, and to promote the study of Sacred Scripture, created the Biblical Commission.

In the encyclical *Immortale Dei* (1885) Leo XIII, who was so deeply engaged in the problem of Church-State relations as they affected France, Germany, and Italy, dwelt on the whole question of what such relations ought properly to be. (*See Document No. 20.*) It was an adaptation to the needs of modern times of the old "Render to Caesar . . . ," and set out the true distinction between Church and State, and of the rights of each over men, who are at once citizens and children of God.

In the encyclical on *Liberty*, Leo criticized the Liberal position on the "modern liberties," and defined clearly the true meaning of liberty and tolerance as distinguished from the wild claims of the age. (*See Document No. 21.*)

Rerum Novarum (1891). The pope's most famous encyclical, however, concerned the condition of the workers. The social problem created by the Industrial

Revolution and economic liberalism had long called for strong Christian action. The Abbé Lammenais had pointed out early in the century the materialistic character of an economic philosophy based on greed. As the Industrial Revolution spread, a new class, the proletariat, exploited, isolated, and without defenders, grew in numbers. It was the century of Karl Marx, whose extreme answer would destroy Christianity, freedom, and private property completely. In 1891 Leo XIII gathered the fruit of some thirty years of discussions and study of the social problem by outstanding Catholic leaders, and published his famous encyclical *On the Condition of the Workers* (*Rerum novarum*). This has become the charter of the Catholic Social movement. (*See Document No. 22.*) It condemned the economic liberalism of those who treated the workers as a commodity to be employed and paid according to the law of supply and demand. It condemned, likewise, the Marxian solution which would make man the helpless instrument of the omnipotent state. It insisted that the worker be paid a living family wage and be permitted to organize to defend his rights and his dignity. To help the worker attain his due the state should intervene in the economic life of the nation.

Pius X.   Leo's successor, Pius X (1903-1914) is the only pope to have been canonized (1954) since Pius V, who died in 1572. This man of such great gentleness and holiness had led a long career as a parish priest and bishop. As pope he was soon faced with a first-rate crisis with France and a subtle pervasive heresy in modernism. Within the Church his measures revitalized its spiritual life.

Leo XIII, as we have seen, had been unable to unite the French Catholics behind his appeal to them to support and Christianize the French Republic. The Dreyfus affair (1894-1906), in which the majority of the Catholics proved to be on the wrong side, stirred up a new bitterness which permitted the anticlerical government of Émile Combes to launch a fierce attack on the religious congregations and the Catholic school system. Diplomatic relations with the Vatican were broken (1904) following the formal visit of the French president to the king of Italy. The next year the government denounced the Concordat of 1801 and proclaimed a complete separation of Church and State. Religious congregations were disbanded and forced to give up their hospitals and schools and to leave the country. The Law of Separation, whereby the government entrusted the management of ecclesiastical property to committees of laymen, was condemned in 1906 by Pius X like the other hostile actions of the government. The French Catholics accepted the tremendous sacrifices at the counsel of the pope who preferred to give up vast properties—churches, schools, houses of clergy—rather than compromise the Church. The separation marked the lowest point in the anti-religious campaign of the Third Republic.

In 1907 Pius X published his famous encyclical *Pascendi* condemning modernism. This was a heresy which had prompted its followers to try to accommodate Catholic dogma and metaphysics to the conclusions of contemporary science by sacrificing traditional dogmatic teaching. The strong condemnation cut short a movement which would have made Catholic theology and philosophy as vague and confused as modernist Protestantism.

Pius X holds a high place for having revitalized Catholic spiritual life and reorganized the machinery of Church government. He encouraged the frequent reception of Holy Communion, restored plain chant to its proper role in religious services, and reformed the Divine Office. By entrusting to the Benedictines the task of revising the text of the Latin Bible and by inaugurating a complete codification of canon law, Pius X showed himself as much aware of the needs of the Church in the twentieth century as he was determined to meet them.

Benedict XV. Pius X was seventy-nine years old when he died in the first month of World War I. As Italy was still neutral, the College of Cardinals was able to meet without any difficulty, and it elected Benedict XV, a man of considerable diplomatic experience. The horrors of the war and the passions it aroused drowned his appeals for peace and mercy. Besieged by each side to declare its cause just, the pope proclaimed his complete neutrality. When conditions suggested the possibility of bringing the exhausting war to an end, he proposed peace terms (*see Document No. 23*), but these were rejected. All during the war Benedict XV devoted himself to works of charity, seeking to effect the exchange of incurably wounded prisoners and to alleviate the lot of the homeless of both sides, facilitating communication between prisoners and their families. Papal charity and neutrality and the roles played by the clergy during the war did much to abate the prewar anticlericalism of Europe. Benedict's successor would profit by the new conditions to settle the Roman question and to renew diplomatic relations with France.

Pius XI. The new pope, Pius XI (1922-1939), was a scholar and a diplomat. In the great Ambrosian Library in Milan and then as prefect of the Vatican Library, Don Ratti had lived the life of a scholar. As papal nuncio to Poland (1918-1921), which had just recovered its independence, he had proved his courage by remaining in Warsaw when its loss to the Communists seemed inevitable.

As the postwar world gradually returned to some sort of order, the new pope used all his diplomatic talents to re-establish normal relations with the new states brought into existence by the Treaty of Versailles and to restore relations with the older states which had broken with the Vatican. In all, eighteen concordats were made by Pius XI.

The fanatical hatred for the papacy which had characterized several of the liberal governments of the nineteenth century gradually subsided in the postwar world. The obvious greatness of the twentieth-century popes, the extraordinary wartime charity of Benedict XV, as well as the conduct of the clergy generally, won a new understanding even from the enemies of the Church. Liberal regimes and dreams were shattered as totalitarian states (Russia, Italy) began to emerge from the chaos produced by the war. Nowhere was the failure of liberalism more evident than in Italy. There the incompetence and corruption of the liberal government collapsed before Mussolini's demand for power. But well before the rise of Mussolini there had been signs of a *rapprochement* between the government of Italy and the Holy See. In 1926 Mussolini took the initiative in arranging for the settlement of the Roman Question, and on February 7, 1929, the Lateran Treaty and Concordat with Italy were officially announced after two years of secret negotiations.

The Lateran Treaty. The Lateran Treaty made Catholicism the state religion of Italy and recognized the pope as ruler of the independent sovereign state of Vatican City—with all the rights and privileges of a temporal ruler. The pope gave up his claim to the former Papal States and received a financial compensation for the surrendered territory. (*See Document No. 24, Part 1.*)

The Concordat. The concordat, which was worked out at the same time, defined Church-State relations and guaranteed the free exercise of the Church's spiritual power—freedom to name bishops and to communicate with the hierarchy of Italy, and freedom for the Catholic press. For the first time in centuries the Church of Italy was free from the control of princes and of the king as regards ecclesiastical appointments and from the suffocating interference of the State. The teaching of Catholic doctrine in the schools and the application of canon law to the sacrament of matrimony were guaranteed. (*See Document 24, Part 2.*) By patience and insistence on essential principles, Pius XI had solved the Roman Question, restored the temporal sovereignty of the papacy, and guaranteed a new era in its history. The treaty and the concordat in no way meant that Pius XI approved of the Fascist regime or its concept of the State, and he did not hesitate to make clear the opposition between the Catholic and Fascist concepts of the State in a strong encyclical, *Non abbiamo bisogno* (1931). (*See Document No. 25.*)

The rise of Hitler's totalitarian state in the 1930's brought the world face to face with naked power, armed with the fruits of modern technology and superb organization. The concordat that Hitler agreed to in 1933 was no sooner signed than it was broken by the chancellor. While the West naively sought to appease the new tyranny, Pius XI boldly called the world's attention to the real nature of this political perversion in his encyclical *Mit brennender Sorge* (March 14, 1937). Several days later, he castigated with equal force the Communist regime of Russia in his encyclical on *Atheistic Communism* (March 19). It was one of a series of condemnations of

Communism dating back to 1846. (*See Document No.
26.*)

These three condemnations of twentieth-century totalitarianism have made abundantly clear the papacy's opposition to amoral political absolutism. Like his modern predecessors, Pius XI resorted to encyclicals to instruct the faithful in their spiritual obligations and to warn them against the evils which beset them. Although these appeals strengthened and united them, they could not prevent the mad race toward war.

Pius XII. When Pius XI died in February 1939 his Secretary of State, Cardinal Pacelli, was elected to succeed him on the first ballot. Like Benedict XV before and during World War I, Pius XII appealed to the world for peace, and when the war came devoted himself unstintingly to mitigating its horrors and succoring its victims. His has been a reign devoted to the work of peace with justice (*see Document No. 27*), as he appeals to statesmen to recognize the need for government by law, the rights of the human person and of nations. (*See Documents Nos. 28 and 29.*) With the faithful he has continued the policy of his predecessors of teaching through encyclicals the need for a deeper spiritual and intellectual life.

As we come to the end of this brief sketch, which in its brevity has had to omit many things, it is clear that the papacy has survived attacks of all kinds made upon it during more than nineteen centuries, from its foundation in the days of the Roman Empire to those of the twentieth-century totalitarian states which have tried to organize a materialistic secular paradise without God or freedom. The modern papacy has witnessed the collapse of three totalitarian states (Italy, Germany, Japan). The fourth, that of Communist Russia, has not yet run its course. Of the outcome in this gigantic struggle between the spiritual freedom of men and their atheistic enslavement there can be no doubt, for in the future as in the past there is the tremendous assurance of the Divine promise: "The gates of hell shall not prevail against it."

Lord Macaulay, the English historian, was prompted to express his admiration for the papacy and the Church in these memorable words:

"The history of the Roman Catholic Church joins together the two great ages of human civilization. No other institution is left standing which carries the mind back to the times when the smoke of sacrifice rose from the Pantheon, and when camelopards and tigers bounded in the Flavian amphitheater. The proudest royal houses are but of yesterday when compared with the line of Supreme Pontiffs. That line we trace back in an unbroken series from the pope who crowned Napoleon in the nineteenth century to the pope who crowned Pepin in the eighth; and far beyond the time of Pepin the august dynasty extends. . . . The republic of Venice came next in antiquity. But the republic of Venice was modern when compared with the Papacy; and the Republic of Venice is gone, and the papacy remains. The papacy remains, not in decay, not a mere antique, but full of life and youthful vigor. . . . Nor do we see any sign which indicates that the term of her [the Church's] long dominion is approaching. She saw the commencement of all the governments and of all the ecclesiastical establishments that now exist in the world; and we feel no assurance that she is not destined to see the end of them all." [1]

[1] Thomas Babington Macaulay, *Critical and Historical Essays, Contributed to the Edinburgh Review* (Leipzig, 1850) IV, 98-99.

Part II

DOCUMENTS

— Document No. 1 —

THE LETTER OF ST. CLEMENT TO THE CORINTHIANS, 95-96 [1]

The long letter of Pope Clement I, written in 95-96, was brought to Corinth by three delegates of the Roman Church who were instructed to return to Rome with confirmation that the schism had been settled. Clement outlines in his letter the constitution of the early Church and points out to the seditious members of the church of Corinth that the powers of the bishops are received from Christ through the Apostles, not from the congregation.

✦ ✦ ✦

The Apostles received the Gospel for us from the Lord Jesus Christ; Jesus Christ was sent from God. Christ, therefore, is from God and the Apostles are from Christ. Both, accordingly, came in proper order by the will of God. Receiving their orders, therefore, and being filled with confidence because of the Resurrection of the Lord Jesus Christ, and confirmed in the word of God, with full assurance of the Holy Spirit, they went forth preaching the Gospel of the Kingdom of God that was about to come. Preaching, accordingly, throughout the country and the cities, they appointed their first-fruits, after testing them by the Spirit, to be bishops and deacons

[1] Francis X. Glimm, "The Letter of St. Clement of Rome to the Corinthians" in Glimm, Marique, and Walsh, *The Apostolic Fathers* (New York, Fathers of the Church, Inc., 1946) pp. 42-54. Reprinted with permission.

of those who should believe. And this they did without innovation, since many years ago things had been written concerning bishops and deacons. Thus the Scripture says in one place: "I will establish their bishops in justice and their deacons in faith." (*Isa. 60.17.*). . . .

Our Apostles also knew, through our Lord Jesus Christ, that there would be contention over the bishop's office. So, for this cause, having received complete foreknowledge, they appointed the above-mentioned men, and afterwards gave them a permanent character, so that, as they died, other approved men should succeed to their ministry. Those, therefore, who were appointed by the Apostles or afterwards by other eminent men, with the consent of the whole Church, and who ministered blamelessly to the flock of Christ in humility, peaceably and nobly, being commended for many years by all— these men we consider are not justly deposed from their ministry. It will be no small sin for us, if we depose from the episcopacy men who have blamelessly and in holiness offered up sacrifice. Blessed are the presbyters who have gone before since they reached a fruitful and perfect end; for now they need not fear that anyone shall remove them from the place assigned to them. For we see that, in spite of their good conduct, you have forced some men from a ministry which they fulfilled without blame. . . .

You, therefore, who laid the foundation of rebellion, submit to the presbyters, and accept chastisement for repentance, bending the knees of your heart. Learn to be submissive, laying aside the boastful and proud self-confidence of your tongue, for it is better for you to be found "little ones," but honorable within the flock of Christ than to seem to be pre-eminent, but to be cast out from His hope. . . . Take our advice, and there will be nothing for you to regret. For, as God lives and the Lord Jesus Christ lives and the Holy Spirit, the faith and hope of the elect, so shall he who with humility of mind, and ready gentleness, and without turning back, has performed the decrees and commandments given by God be enrolled and chosen among the number of those who are saved through Jesus Christ. . . . But, if some shall disobey the words which have been spoken by Him through us, let them know that they will involve themselves in no small transgression and danger. But we shall be innocent of this sin. . . .

— Document No. 2 —

THE LETTER OF ST. IGNATIUS TO THE ROMANS[2]

St. Ignatius, third Bishop of Antioch, while on his way to Rome to be martyred, wrote seven letters, six to the Christians of six different communities and one to Poly-carp, Bishop of Smyrna. In his letter to the Romans he recognizes the special position of the Roman Church over the others.

✓   ✓   ✓

Ignatius Theophorus to the Church on which the majesty of the most high Father and of Jesus Christ, His only Son, has had mercy; to the Church beloved and enlightened by the faith and charity of Jesus Christ, our God, through the will of Him who has willed all things that exist—the Church in the place of the country of the Romans which holds the primacy. I salute you in the name of Jesus Christ, the Son of the Father. You are a Church worthy of God, worthy of honor, felicitation and praise, worthy of attaining to God, a Church without blemish, which holds the primacy of the community of love, obedient to Christ's law, bearing the Father's name. To you who are united, outwardly and inwardly, in the whole of His commandment and filled with grace, in union with God and with every alien stain filtered away, I wish every innocent joy in Jesus Christ, our God. . . . Never have you envied anyone. You have been others' teachers. I trust that what you have taught and pre-scribed to others may now be applied by yourselves. . . .

[2] Gerald G. Walsh, "The Letters of St. Ignatius of Antioch" in Glimm, Marique, and Walsh, *The Apostolic Fathers* (New York, Fathers of the Church, Inc., 1946) pp. 107-109.

— Document No. 3 —

THE POSITION OF ST. IRENAEUS ON THE PRIMACY OF ROME[3]

Brought up in Asia Minor and taught the faith by Poly-
carp, bishop of Smyrna, who had received it directly
from the Apostles, St. Irenaeus is the most important
witness of the second century. His great work Against
Heresies is the oldest treatise on the Church. In the pas-
sage below he stresses the primacy of the Roman Church,
and the importance of the oral tradition given to the
Apostles and their successors, the bishops.

ᕙ   ᕙ   ᕙ

But as it would be exceedingly long to enumerate in
such a work as this the succession [of bishops] in all the
churches [we shall limit ourselves] to that of the greatest
and oldest church, the one known to all, founded and
established at Rome by the two most glorious apostles
Peter and Paul. By showing that this is the one which
has from the Apostles the tradition and faith proclaimed
to men by successive bishops down to our own day we
shall confound all those who in any way whatsoever,
either to please themselves or through vainglory, blind-
ness, or bad judgment, assemble for worship otherwise
than they ought.

With this church, on account of its greater authority,
every church must agree—that is the faithful everywhere
—for the tradition which has come down from the
Apostles in this church has always been preserved by
the faithful everywhere.

[3] Translated by the author from the Latin text edited by
F. Sagnard, *Irénée de Lyon contre les hérésies* (Paris,
1952).

After founding and organizing the Church, the blessed Apostles transmitted to Linus the episcopate. This is the Linus mentioned by St. Paul in his letters to Timothy. Anacletus succeeded him. Then the episcopate fell to Clement, third in line after the Apostles. He had seen the Apostles themselves and conferred with them. He had heard their preaching and beheld the tradition from them before his eyes. He was not alone in this, for there were still many in his time who had been taught by the Apostles. During the reign of Clement there arose a rather serious dissension among the brethren at Corinth. The Roman church wrote a very important letter to the Corinthians urging them to make peace, to restore their faith and to proclaim the tradition which it had lately received from the Apostles. . . . (*See Document No. 1.*)

Evaristus succeeded Clement, and Alexander, Evaristus; then Sixtus became the sixth from the Apostles, and after him Telesphorus, who died gloriously a martyr. Then in turn Hyginus, Pius, and Anicetus; Soter succeeded Anicetus. Eleutherius, now reigning, is the twelfth bishop from the Apostles.

It is in this order and through this succession that the tradition, which is in the Church from the Apostles, and the preaching of truth has come down to us. This is a complete demonstration that this life-giving faith is the one and the same which has been preserved in the Church and handed down in truth from the Apostles. . . .

If a dispute arises on some minor point, should one not have recourse to the oldest churches, those in which the Apostles lived, to learn from them what is certain and clear about the question at issue? What if the Apostles had not left us the Scriptures? Would we not be obliged to follow the order of tradition which they handed on to those to whom they entrusted the churches?

For this is what many barbarians who believe in Christ have done. Without parchment or ink, they have salvation "written in their hearts by the Holy Spirit" (*II Cor. 3.3*) and keep the old tradition diligently, believing in one God, Creator of heaven and earth and all it contains. . . .

— Document No. 4 —

THE EMPERORS THEODOSIUS II AND VALENTINIAN III RECOGNIZE THE PRIMACY OF ROME, 445 [4]

Hilary, Bishop of Arles, was condemned by Pope Leo I for deposing a subordinate bishop without consulting the Holy See. When Hilary protested the papal intervention, the emperors Theodosius and Valentinian ordered use of imperial force to impose acceptance. The fragment of the imperial edict (445) given below shows how clearly these two emperors recognized papal jurisdiction over all the bishops of the Church and the way civil power was used to support papal rights in the name of public order.

✓   ✓   ✓

It is clear that for us and for our Empire the only support is in the favour of the Supreme Godhead; to merit this we must assist in the first place the Christian faith and venerable religion. Since therefore the merit of St. Peter, who is the prince of the episcopal crown, the dignity of the City of Rome and the authority of a holy synod have established the primacy of the Apostolic See, let not presumption attempt to carry out anything contrary to the authority of that See; for then at last the peace of the Church will be preserved everywhere, if the whole body recognizes its ruler. . . . We decree by this perpetual Edict that it will not be lawful for the bishops of Gaul or of other provinces to attempt anything contrary to ancient custom without the authority of that venerable man the Pope of the Eternal City. But let whatever the authority of the Apostolic See decrees or shall decree, be accepted as law by all.

[4] Sidney Z. Ehler and John B. Morrall, *Church and State through the Centuries* (Westminster, Maryland, The Newman Press, 1954) pp. 7-9. Reprinted with permission.

— Document No. 5 —

POPE GELASIUS I ON CHURCH-STATE RELATIONS, 494[5]

*Pope Gelasius I (492-496) protested the interference of
the Byzantine emperor Anastasius (491-518) in ecclesiastical affairs in a famous letter (494), in which he distinguished between the spiritual and temporal powers.
The letter, of which a fragment is given below, was
frequently referred to by both sides in medieval con-
troversies between pope and emperor.*

✓　　　　✓　　　　✓

I beg Your Piety not to consider as arrogance what
is a duty in keeping with the Divine plan. Far be it from
a Roman princeps to take offense at the truth made
known to him. There are two [powers], August Emperor,
by which this world is chiefly governed: the sacred authority of the pontiffs and the royal power. Of the two
the charge of the priests is heavier, in that they have to
render an account in the Divine judgment for even the
kings of men. For you know, most gracious son, that,
though you preside over humankind by virtue of your
office, you bow your neck piously to those who are in
charge of things divine and from them you ask the things
of your salvation; and hence you realize that in receiving the heavenly mysteries and making proper arrangement for them, you must in the order of religion submit
yourself rather than control, and that in these matters

[5] Aloysius K. Ziegler, "Pope Gelasius I and His Teaching on
the Relations of Church and State," *The Catholic Historical Review,* Vol. 27 (1942) pp. 412-437. Reprinted with
permission.

you are dependent on their judgment and do not desire them to be subject to your will. For if, as far as the sphere of civil order is concerned, the bishops themselves, recognizing that the imperial office has been conferred upon you by Divine disposition, obey your laws . . . with what zeal, I ask you, should you not obey those who are deputed to dispense the sacred mysteries? Moreover, as no light peril threatens pontiffs who have kept silence in what concerns the worship of God, so there is no little danger for those, who, God forbid, show contempt when they should obey. And if the hearts of the faithful should in principle bow before all priests who rightly discharge divine functions, how much more must they give their assent to the head of that see whom the highest Divinity wished to rank above all priests and whom the piety of the universal Church has subsequently ever held in honor. As Your Piety is well aware no one can ever by any human device elevate himself to the privilege and confession of him whom the word of Christ set before all, whom the venerable Church has always confessed and devoutly holds as its primate. The things which are instituted by Divine judgment can be attacked by human presumption, but they can be overcome by the power of none. . . .

— Document No. 6 —

CHARLEMAGNE ON CHURCH-STATE RELATIONS, 796[6]

The following extract from a letter of Charlemagne, written to Pope Leo III in 796, indicates the Carolingian king's concept of the function of the pope. By limiting the pope's role to prayer Charlemagne reserves to himself the task of defending the Church and of strengthening "within it the knowledge of the Catholic Faith."

✓ ✓ ✓

Just as I entered into a pact with the most blessed father your predecessor, so I desire to conclude with your Holiness an unbreakable treaty of the same faith and charity; so that with Divine grace being called down by the prayers of your Apostolic Sanctity, the Apostolic benediction may follow me everywhere, and the most holy See of the Roman Church may always be defended by the devotion which God gives to us. It is our part with the help of Divine holiness to defend by armed strength the holy Church of Christ everywhere from the outward onslaught of the pagans and the ravages of the infidels, and to strengthen within it the knowledge of the Catholic Faith. It is your part, most holy Father, to help our armies with your hands lifted up to God like Moses, so that by your intercession and by the leadership and gift of God the Christian people may everywhere and always have the victory over the enemies of His Holy Name and that the name of our Lord Jesus Christ may be glorified throughout the whole world.

[6] Ehler and Morrall, *op. cit.*, p. 12.

— Document No. 7 —

DECREE OF POPE NICHOLAS II ON PAPAL ELECTIONS, 1059[7]

A fundamental step in freeing the Papacy from imperial control was the decree (1059) of Pope Nicholas II (1058-1061) reserving the election of the pope to the cardinals. The paragraph, in which the pope recognizes vaguely the rights of Henry IV, was omitted when the decree was reissued in 1060.

✓   ✓   ✓

. . . Strengthened by the authority of our predecessors and of other holy Fathers, we decide and decree:

That, when the Pontiff of this Universal Roman Church dies, the Cardinal-Bishops shall first take counsel with most diligent consideration, thereupon call in to themselves the Cardinal-Clerics and then, in the same manner, the remaining clergy and people shall approach to express their consent to the new election.

That—to be sure that the disease of venality will have no opportunity to creep in—the churchmen shall have the leading part in effecting the election of the Pope, and the others shall only be followers. . . .

Let them make their choice from the Roman Church itself, if a suitable person is to be found there; if not, a person from elsewhere may be elected.

Saving due honour and reverence for our beloved son Henry, who is at present called king and who, if God wills, is expected to be future emperor; in so far as we have made such concessions to himself and his successors,

[7] Ehler and Morrall, *op. cit.*, pp. 26-27.

who shall personally have obtained this right from this holy Apostolic See.

But if the perversity of corrupt and evil men shall so prevail, that an uncorrupted, genuine and free election may not be made in the City, the Cardinal-Bishops together with the clerics of the Church and Catholic laity, however few, may be legally empowered to elect a Pontiff to the Apostolic See wherever they shall judge to be more suitable.

After an election shall have been definitely made, if a warlike disturbance or the attempt of any man whatever who may be inspired by an evil disposition, shall not allow the person who has been elected to the Apostolic See to be enthroned according to custom, nevertheless the person elected shall, as Pope, obtain authority to rule the Roman church and to dispose of all its prerogatives, as we know blessed Gregory did before his consecration.

But if anyone, contrary to this our statute promulgated by decision of the Synod, shall by discord or usurpation or any trickery whatsoever be elected, consecrated and enthroned, let him be held and accounted by all not as Pope but as Satan, not as an Apostle but as an apostate. . . .

THE *DICTATUS PAPAE* OF GREGORY VII[8]

The Dictatus Papae, found in the register of the official letters of Gregory VII (1073-1085), seems to be a summary of the principles guiding Gregorian reformers.

1. That the Roman Church was founded by God alone.
2. That the Roman Pontiff alone is rightly to be called universal.
3. That he alone can depose or reinstate bishops.
4. That his legate, even if of lower grade, takes precedence, in a council, of all bishops and may render a sentence of deposition against them.
5. That the pope may depose the absent.
6. That, among other things, we also ought not to stay in the same house with those excommunicated by him.
7. That for him alone it is lawful to enact new laws according to the needs of the time, to assemble together new congregations, to make an abbey of a canonry; and on the other hand to divide a rich bishopric and to unite the poor ones.
8. That he alone may use the imperial insignia.
9. That the pope is the only one whose feet are to be kissed by all princes.
10. That his name alone is to be recited in churches.
11. That his title is unique in the world.
12. That he may depose emperors.

[8] Ehler and Morrall, *op. cit.*, pp. 43-44.

13. That he may transfer bishops, if necessary, from one See to another.
14. That he has the power to ordain a cleric of any Church he may wish.
15. That he who has been ordained by him may rule over another church, but not be under the command of others; and that such a one may not receive a higher grade from any bishop.
16. That no synod may be called a general one without his order.
17. That no chapter or book may be regarded as canonical without his authority.
18. That no sentence of his may be retracted by anyone; and that he, alone of all, can retract it.
19. That he himself may be judged by no one.
20. That no one shall dare to condemn a person who appeals to the Apostolic See.
21. That to this See the more important cases of every Church should be submitted.
22. That the Roman Church has never erred, nor ever, by the witness of Scripture, shall err to all eternity.
23. That the Roman Pontiff, if canonically ordained, is undoubtedly sanctified by the merits of St. Peter. . . .
24. That, by his order and with his permission, subordinate persons may bring accusations.
25. That without convening a synod he can depose and reinstate bishops.
26. That he should not be considered as Catholic who is not in conformity with the Roman Church.
27. That the pope may absolve subjects of unjust men from their fealty.

— Document No. 9 —

THE CONCORDAT OF WORMS, 1122[9]

The Concordat of Worms, agreed to in 1122 by Pope Callistus II and the Emperor Henry V, settled the lay investiture controversy which had so long plagued the Church. In it each party states separately the concessions made to the other.

✦   ✦   ✦

I, bishop Calixtus [Callistus], servant of the servants of God, concede to you, beloved son Henry—by the grace of God August Emperor of the Romans—that the election of those bishops and abbots in the German kingdom who belong to the kingdom shall take place in your presence without simony and without any violence; so that if any discord occurs between the parties concerned, you may with the counsel and judgment of the metropolitan and the co-provincials—give your assent and assistance to the party which appears to have the better case. The candidate elected may receive the *regalia* from you through the sceptre and he shall perform his lawful duties to you for them. But he who is elected in the other parts of the Empire shall, within six months, receive the *regalia* from you through the sceptre and shall perform his lawful duties for them, saving all things which are known as pertaining to the Church. If you complain to me in any of these matters and ask for help, I will furnish you the aid, if such is the duty of

[9] Ehler and Morrall, *op. cit.,* pp. 48-49.

my office, I grant true peace to you and to all those who are or have been of your party during this discord.

Privilege of the Emperor:

I, Henry, by the grace of God August Emperor of the Romans, for the love of God and of the Holy Roman Church and of the lord Pope Calixtus and for the healing of my soul, do surrender to God, to the Holy Apostles of God, Peter and Paul, and to the Holy Roman Church all investiture through ring and staff; and do agree that in all churches throughout my kingdom and empire there shall be canonical elections and free consecrations. I restore to the same Roman Church all the possessions and temporalities [*regalia*] which have been abstracted until the present day either in the lifetime of my father or in my own and which I hold; and I will faithfully aid in the restoration of those which I do not hold. The possessions also of all other churches and princes and of everyone else, either cleric or layman, which had been lost in that war, I will restore, so far as I hold them, according to the counsel of the princes or according to justice; and I will faithfully aid in the restoration of those that I do not hold. And I grant a true peace to the lord Pope Calixtus and to the Holy Roman Church and to all who are or have been on its side. In matters where the Holy Roman Church would seek assistance I will faithfully grant it; and in those where she shall complain to me I will duly grant justice to her.

— Document No. 10 —

DECREE OF POPE ALEXANDER III ON PAPAL ELECTIONS, 1179[10]

Because of continued trouble over papal elections and the support of antipopes by minority groups, Alexander III (1159-1181) amended the decree of Nicholas II (see Document No. 7) in order to overcome the difficulty at the Third General Council of the Lateran in 1179.

↗   ↗   ↗

Although ordinances have emanated from our predecessors which are clear enough and destined to prevent any discord, nonetheless grave splits often occurred in the Church after these ordinances, due to the audacity of wicked ambition; in order to avoid this evil, we, too, have decided to make some addition to them, by the advice of our brothers and by the approval of the holy Council.

We therefore decree that if, by any chance, full concord could not be achieved in view of constituting a Pontiff, owing to a hostile man sowing tares of discord among the Cardinals, and one-third of them would not be willing to agree with the two other thirds united and concordant, or even would presume to consecrate some other candidate, he shall be regarded as Roman Pontiff who shall be elected and received by two-thirds.

But if any one, relying on the nomination by one-third, shall usurp for himself the episcopal name—for the substance of the episcopal function he cannot usurp—he himself and those who shall have received him shall be subject to excommunication. . . .

[10] Ehler and Morrall, *op. cit.,* pp. 63-64.

— Document No. 11 —

POPE INNOCENT III'S INTERVEN-
TION *RATIONE PECCATI*, 1204[11]

When John Lackland, king of England, appealed to Pope Innocent III against Philip Augustus, king of France, the pope justified in the decretal, Novit ille (1204) his right to intervene in the war between France and England in order to re-establish peace.

↗   ↗   ↗

No one, therefore, may suppose that we intend to disturb or diminish the jurisdiction or power of the illustrious king of the French just as he himself does not want to and should not impede our jurisdiction and power; as we are insufficient to discharge all our jurisdiction, why should we wish to usurp that of anyone else? . . . For we do not intend to render justice in feudal matters, in which the jurisdiction belongs to him, unless something may be detracted from the common law by some special privilege or contrary custom, but we want to decide in the matter of sins, of which the censure undoubtedly pertains to us and we can and must exercise it against any one.

In this, indeed, we do not lean on human constitutions, but much more on Divine Law, because our power is not from man but from God: any one who has a sound mind knows that it belongs to our office to draw away any Christian from any mortal sin and, if he despises the correction, to coerce him with ecclesiastical penalties.

[11] Ehler and Morrall, *op. cit.*, pp. 69-70.

— Document No. 12 —

PIUS II'S CONDEMNATION OF CONCILIARISM, 1460[12]

The conciliar theory, which claimed that a general council of the Church was the supreme authority in the Church, died hard. Those who could not obtain what they wanted from the pope would appeal to a future council—a practice which tended to destroy the pope's legal authority. Although Pope Pius II condemned the theory in the bull Execrabilis *(1460), the practice continued: Luther, for example, in 1520 appealed to a council after the pope condemned his teaching.*

An execrable, and in former ages unheard-of abuse, has sprung up in our time, namely that some people, imbued with the spirit of rebellion, presume to appeal to a future Council from the Roman pontiff, the Vicar of Jesus Christ, to whom it was said in the person of blessed Peter: "Feed my sheep" and "Whatsoever thou shalt bind on earth shall be bound also in Heaven"; they do not do so because they are anxious to obtain a sounder judgment, but in order to escape the consequences of their sins, and anyone who is not ignorant of the laws can realize how contrary this is to the sacred canons and how detrimental to the Christian community. Because—passing over other things which are most manifestly opposed to this corruption—who would not find it ridiculous when appeals are made to what does not

[12] Ehler and Morrall, *op. cit.*, pp. 131-133.

exist and the time of whose future existence nobody knows? The poor are oppressed in many ways by the stronger, crimes remain unpunished, freedom is conceded to delinquents, and all the ecclesiastical discipline and hierarchical order is confounded.

Wishing therefore to thrust away from Christ's Church this pestilent venom, to take care of the salvation of all those who have been committed to us, and to hold off from the sheepfold of our Saviour all cause of scandal, we condemn appeals of this kind by the counsel of all prelates and jurisconsults of Divine and human law adhering to the Curia and on the ground of our sure knowledge; and we denounce them as erroneous and detestable, quash and entirely annul them in the event that any such appeals, extant at present, may be discovered, and we declare and determine that they are—like something void and pestilent—of no significance. Consequently, we enjoin that nobody dares under whatever pretext to make such an appeal from any of our ordinances, sentences or commands and from those of our successors, or to adhere to such appeals, made by others, or to use them in any manner.

If anyone, of whatever status, rank, order or condition he may be, even if adorned with Imperial, royal or Papal dignity, shall contravene this after the space of two months from the day of the publication of this Bull by the Apostolic Chancery, he shall *ipso facto* incur sentence of anathema, from which he can not be absolved except by the Roman Pontiff and at the point of death. A University or a corporation shall be subjected to an ecclesiastical interdict; nonetheless, corporations and Universities, like the aforesaid and any other persons, shall incur those penalties and censures which offenders who have committed the *crimen laesae maiestatis* and promoters of heretical depravity are known to incur. Furthermore scriveners and witnesses who shall witness acts of this kind and, in general, all those who shall knowingly furnish counsel, help or favor to such appealers, shall be punished with the same penalty.

THE CONCORDAT OF BOLOGNA, 1516[13]

*The Concordat of Bologna (August 18, 1516) was ap-
proved by the Fifth Lateran Council which was in
session at the time the concordat was made. The principal
provisions of the concordat, given below, are taken from
the bull* Primitiva illa ecclesia *of Leo X.*

✓   ✓   ✓

We have been turning over in our inmost mind the
dealings which took place between our predecessors, the
Roman Pontiffs of pious memory, Pius II, Sixtus IV,
Innocent VIII, Alexander VI and Julius II, and the
most Christain Kings of France of illustrious memory,
concerning the abrogation of a certain enactment known
as the "Pragmatic [Sanction]," in force in the kingdom
of France; and although the aforesaid Pius II sent ambassadors to Louis XI . . . and by force of argument
exercised persuasion on him so that the same king by
his letters patent abrogated this Pragmatic Sanction, as
a thing originating in sedition and brought forth at a time
of schism, nevertheless this abrogation was not carried
out; and also special Apostolic letters of the aforesaid
Sixtus, our predecessor, concerning the things agreed between the ambassadors of the said King Louis and the
above-mentioned Sixtus were not accepted by the prelates
and ecclesiastical persons of the aforesaid kingdom when
they were sent to them; these same prelates and ecclesiastical persons would not obey them, nor did they give

---

[13] Ehler and Morrall, *op. cit.*, pp. 137-141.

heed to the warnings of the said Innocent and Julius, but wished to adhere to the same Pragmatic enactment. Therefore our predecessor Julius, in the present Lateran Council, lawfully summoned by him to represent the Universal Church, committed the accomplishment of the task of abrogating this Pragmatic Sanction and the discussion of it to the assemblies of his venerable brethren the Cardinals, of whose number we ourselves then were, and of other prelates, and ordered that the result of these deliberations should be communicated to himself and to the same Council. The French prelates . . . of whatever dignity they might be, even if royal, who practiced the aforesaid Sanction or approved of it, were to be warned by public edict . . . and cited . . . to present themselves before the Pope in the aforesaid Council and to give reasons why the said Sanction should not be declared pronounced and abrogated as null and void in its provisions concerning the authority, dignity and unity of the Roman Church and the Apostolic See and the violation of the sacred Canons and ecclesiastical liberty.

After the matter had been dealt with in legal form in the abovementioned Lateran Council and our predecessor Julius II had been, according to God's pleasure, removed from human affairs, we also . . . proceeded to certain acts against these prelates, Chapters, assemblies and persons with the ultimate consideration that peace is the bond of charity. . . . Then we have learnt by exhaustive discussions . . . when we discussed these things in His Majesty's presence and exhorted him with paternal advice, that the King was willing, to the praise of God and his own honour, to abrogate freely, willingly and with ready mind the aforesaid Pragmatic Sanction, to live according to the laws of the Holy Roman Church, as do other Christians, and to submit to and obey the reservations, expectative graces, Apostolic decrees and provisions which are published from time to time by the Apostolic See.

Grave dangers to souls have arisen from the elections which have been held in cathedral and metropolitan churches and monasteries of the said kingdom. Many of them took place with abuse of secular power, some were preceded by unlawful and simoniacal pacts, others were stained with favoritism and ties of kinship, not without the guilt of perjury for the electors themselves. . . . Therefore King Francis, wishing as a truly obedient son to follow our paternal advice . . . accepted—in place of the aforesaid Pragmatic Sanction and the respective chapters contained in it—the laws and constitutions set out in detail below. . . . We decree and ordain that in the future the rules following hereafter are to be observed perpetually in the said Kingdom, in Dauphiné and the County of Die and Valence in place of the above-mentioned Pragmatic constitution and all the chapters contained in it.

In cathedral and metropolitan churches of the said Kingdom Dauphiné and County, falling vacant now and in the future, even by voluntary cession into our hands and those of our successors canonically succeeding as Roman Pontiffs, their Chapters and Canons shall not proceed to the election or postulations of a future prelate to the diocese but, on the occurrence of such vacancies, the reigning King of France shall, within six months reckoned from the day when the benefice fell vacant, nominate to ourselves and our successors the Roman Pontiffs or to the aforesaid See, a respectable Master or Licentiate in Theology, or a Doctor in both laws or in either Law (Civil or Canon) or a Licentiate who has passed a strict examination in a well-known university, has reached the age of at least twenty-seven years and is otherwise suitable; the person nominated in this way by the King shall be provided by us or our successors or the aforesaid See. If it should happen that the King should nominate a person without such qualifications to the said churches falling vacant in this way, the person so nominated ought not to be provided to the same churches by ourselves and our successors or the See. But the King is bound, within three more months reckoned from the day of rejection of the unqualified person . . . to nominate another person who has the qualifications mentioned above; otherwise, in order that there may be speedy provision for the drawbacks which arise for churches vacant in this manner, the churches thus vacant shall be freely provided by us or our successors, or the same See with a person having the above qualifications. There always shall be free provisions with no preceding nominations by the King in the case of churches vacant by death at the aforesaid See [sc. *in curia*]. We declare that attempted elections violating the above conditions, as well as provisions made against it by ourselves and our successors or the See are null and invalid.

[The same conditions as those given above applied in monasteries and conventual priories where elections were customary.]

We do not intend, however, to prejudice in any respect by this enactment the Chapters of churches and convents of monasteries and priories, who have obtained privileges of electing their own prelate from the Apostolic See; so they may freely proceed to the election of bishops, abbots and priors, according to the privileges conceded to them and the mode laid down in their privileges. . . .

We also will and decree that in the aforesaid Kingdom, Dauphiné and County in future no expectative graces may be given and no special or general reservations to vacant benefices may be made by ourselves and the said See; and if, by reason of pressure or any other reason, they may *de facto* issue from ourselves and our successors and the said See, we declare them to be null and void.

In cathedral, metropolitan or collegiate churches whose statures expressly guarantee that nobody can obtain a personal or administrative dignity or other office in them unless he holds there the effective rank of Canon, we intend to create Canons for the purpose of obtaining such personal or administrative dignities or offices even without waiting for a vacancy.

— Document No. 14 —

THE FOUR GALLICAN ARTICLES, 1682 [14]

The Four Gallican Articles, drawn up by Bishop Bossuet, were adopted by an assembly of seventy-one members of the French clergy in 1682 at the demand of the government. Gallicanism remained a strong force in France in spite of papal condemnation (1690).

✓ ✓ ✓

1. Power has been conferred by God on blessed Peter and his successors, Vicars of Christ Himself, a power over the spiritual things of the Church and those which pertain to eternal salvation, but not over civil and temporal matters. For the Lord Himself said: "My kingdom is not of this world," and again: "Render therefore to Caesar the things that are Caesar's and to God the things that are God's." The Apostle also states his opinion as follows: "Let every soul be subject to higher powers, for there is no power but from God, and those that are ordained by God. Therefore he that resisteth the power resisteth the ordinance of God." Consequently kings and princes are not subjected by the ordinance of God to any ecclesiastical authority in temporal affairs; nor by the authority of the keys of the Church can they be deposed, directly or indirectly, nor can their subjects be dispensed from loyalty and obedience or absolved from the oath of fidelity which they have taken. This judgment is to be universally held as necessary to public quietness, useful to the Church as well as to secular authority and

[14] Ehler and Morrall, *op. cit.*, pp. 207-208.

agreeable to the word of God, the tradition of the Fathers, and the examples of the Saints.

2. Full authority in spiritual matters is, however, inherent in the Apostolic See and the successors of Peter the Vicar of Christ, while at the same time the decrees of the Holy General Council of Constance (passed in its fourth and fifth sessions), concerning the authority of General Councils, are to remain valid and unchanged, approved, as they are, by the Apostolic See and by the practice of the Roman Pontiffs themselves and of the whole Church; nor may the Gallican Church give approval to those who minimize the force of those decrees, as if they were of doubtful authority and little backing, or who disparage the statements of the Council as referring only to the time of schism.

3. Hence the exercise of the Apostolic authority should be moderated by the Canons established by the Holy Spirit and consecrated by the respect of the whole world. Also the rules, customs and institutions accepted in the French kingdom and Church are to keep their force and the bounds fixed by our fathers are to remain undisturbed; for it is essential for the dignity of the Apostolic See, that the statutes and customs, confirmed by the consent of that See itself and of the churches, should enjoy their rightful stability.

4. In questions of faith the leading role is to be that of the Supreme Pontiff; and his decrees apply to all churches in general and to each of them in particular. But his judgment is not unchangeable, unless it receives the consent of the Church.

These are the maxims which we have received from our fathers and which we have decided to send to all the Gallican churches and to the bishops whom the Holy Spirit has installed there to govern them, in order that we may all say the same thing, that we may share the same opinions and all hold the same doctrine.

— Document No. 15 —

THE CIVIL CONSTITUTION
OF THE CLERGY, 1790[15]

*The Civil Constitution of the Clergy, whereby the Na-
tional Constituent Assembly sought to reorganize unilat-
erally the Church in France, caused a bitter split in
France. To force acceptance the National Constituent
Assembly obliged the clergy to take an oath to accept
the Civil Constitution. Pius VI condemned both the Civil
Constitution and the obligation to take an oath in his
bull* Caritas *(1790). The religious conflict and persecution
of the Church lasted until religious peace was restored
by the Concordat of 1801.*

⚹   ⚹   ⚹

The National Assembly, having heard the report of
its Ecclesiastical Committee, has decreed and does decree
the following as constitutional articles.

TITLE I—OF ECCLESIASTICAL OFFICES

1. Each and every department shall constitute a single
diocese, and each and every diocese shall have the same
extent and limits as the department.

2. . . . All bishoprics in the eighty-three departments
which are not included by name in the present article are
and shall forever remain suppressed. . . .

4. No church or parish of France, and no French
citizen may, under any circumstances or on any pretext
whatsoever, acknowledge the authority of an ordinary

---

[15] John Hall Stewart, *A Documentary Survey of the French
Revolution* (New York, The Macmillan Company, 1951)
pp. 169-178. Reprinted with the permission of The Macmillan Company.

bishop or archbishop whose see is established under the name of a foreign power, or that of its delegates residing in France or elsewhere; without prejudice, however, to the unity of faith and communion, which shall be maintained with the Visible Head of the Universal Church as hereinafter provided. . . .

6. A new organization and division of all parishes of the kingdom shall be undertaken immediately, upon the advice of the diocesan bishop and the district administrations; the number and extent thereof shall be determined according to rules to be established. . . .

15. In all cities and towns of not more than 6,000 inhabitants there shall be only one parish; other parishes shall be suppressed and united with the principal church. . . .

20. All titles and offices, other than those mentioned in the present constitution, dignities, canonries, prebends, half prebends, chapels chaplaincies, in both cathedral and collegiate churches, and all regular and secular chapters of either sex, abbeys and priories, regular or *in commendam,* of either sex, and all other benefices and *prestimonies* in general, of whatever kind and under whatever denomination, are abolished and suppressed dating from the day of publication of the present decree, and similar ones may never be established. . . .

TITLE II—OF APPOINTMENTS TO BENEFICES

1. Dating from the day of publication of the present decree, appointments to bishoprics and cures are to be made by election only.

2. All elections shall be by ballot and absolute majority of votes.

3. The election of bishops shall take place according to the form prescribed by, and by the electoral body designated in, the decree of December 22, 1789, for the appointment of members of the departmental assembly.

4. As soon as the departmental *procureur-général-syndic* receives news of a vacancy in an episcopal see, owing to death, resignation or other cause, he shall notify the district *procureurs-syndics* to convoke the electors who effected the last election of members of

the administrative assembly; and at the same time he shall indicate the day on which the election of the bishop shall take place, which shall be not later than the third Sunday after the letter of notification.

5. If the vacancy in the episcopal see occurs during the last four months of the year in which the election of members of the departmental administration is to take place, the election of the bishop shall be deferred and assigned to the next assembly of electors.

6. The election of the bishop may take place or be initiated only on a Sunday, in the principal church of the chief town of the department, following the parochial mass, at which all electors are required to be present.

7. To be eligible for a bishopric, one must have performed for at least fifteen years the duties of ecclesiastical ministry in the diocese, in the capacity of curé, officiating minister or vicar, or as superior or directing vicar of the seminary.

8. Bishops whose sees are suppressed by the present decree may be elected to bishoprics now vacant, as well as to those which become vacant hereafter or which are established in some departments, even if they had not been in office fifteen years. . . .

14. Proclamation of those elected shall be made by the president of the electoral assembly, in the church where the election was held, in the presence of the people and the clergy, and before beginning the solemn mass which is to be celebrated on such occasion.

15. The *procès-verbal* of the election and of the proclamation shall be sent to the King by the president of the assembly of electors to inform His Majesty of the choice that has been made. . . .

19. The new bishop may not apply to the Pope for confirmation, but shall write to him as the Visible Head of the Universal Church, in testimony of the unity of faith and communion which he is to maintain therewith. . . .

21. Before the ceremony of consecration begins, the bishop-elect shall take a solemn oath, in the presence of the municipal officials, the people, and the clergy, to watch with care over the faithful of the diocese entrusted to him, to be faithful to the nation, to the law,

and to the king, and to maintain with all his power the Constitution decreed by the National Assembly and accepted by the King. . . .

25. The election of curés shall be conducted according to the forms prescribed by, and by the electors designated in, the decree of December 22, 1789, for the election of members of the district assembly. . . .

28. The election of curés shall be effected by a separate balloting for each vacant living. . . .

36. The bishop shall have the privilege of examining the curé-elect, in the presence of his council, concerning his doctrine and morals; if he deems him competent, he shall bestow canonical institution; if he believes it his duty to refuse it, the reasons for refusal shall be given in writing signed by the bishop and his council, reserving to the parties recourse to civil authority as hereinafter provided. . . .

38. The curés elected and instituted shall take the same oath as the bishops, on a Sunday in their Church before the parochial mass, in the presence of the municipal officials, the people and the clergy. Until such time, they may not perform any curial function. . . .

40. Bishoprics and livings shall be considered vacant until those elected have taken the oath mentioned.

— Document No. 16 —

THE PENALTIES FOR REFUSING TO TAKE THE OATH TO THE CIVIL CONSTITUTION, 1790[16]

In November 1790 the National Assembly, as a test of loyalty to the revolutionary reorganization of the Church, ordered members of the clergy to take the oath proscribed in Articles 21 and 38 above. (See Document No. 15.) *Penalties for failure to take the oath or to keep it are prescribed as follows.*

5. Those of the said bishops, former archbishops, curés and other ecclesiastical public functionaries who have not, within the established periods, taken the oath prescribed for them respectively shall be deemed to have renounced their office, and provision shall be made for their replacement, as in the case of vacancy by resignation. . . .

6. In case the said bishops, former archbishops, curés and other ecclesiastical public functionaries, after having taken their respective oaths, fail therein, either by refusing to obey the decrees of the National Assembly accepted or sanctioned by the King, or by constituting or instigating opposition to their execution, they shall be prosecuted in the district courts as rebels resisting the law, and punished by deprivation of their stipend, and moreover they shall be declared to have forfeited the rights of active citizenship and to be ineligible for any public office. . . .

[16] Stewart, *op. cit.*, pp. 183-184.

7. Those of the said bishops, former archbishops, curés and other ecclesiastical public functionaries maintained in office and refusing to take their respective oaths, as well as those who have been suppressed, together with the members of secular ecclesiastical bodies likewise suppressed, who enter upon any of their public duties or those which they perform in a body, shall be prosecuted as disturbers of public order and punished with the same penalties as above.

8. All ecclesiastical or lay persons who unite to contrive a refusal to obey the decrees of the National Assembly accepted or sanctioned by the King, or to constitute or instigate opposition to the execution thereof, likewise shall be prosecuted as disturbers of public order, and punished according to the rigor of the laws.

— Document No. 17 —

POPE PIUS VI'S CONDEMNATION OF THE CIVIL CONSTITUTION OF THE CLERGY, 1791 [17]

Pope Pius VI condemned the Civil Constitution in the bull Caritas *issued April 13, 1791. The bull placed the pope on the side of those who refused to accept the Civil Constitution or to swear the oath and produced the deadlock which lasted until the Concordat of 1801.*

✓   ✓   ✓

. . . In a letter dated July 9, 1790, to Louis our son most dear in Christ, a most Christian king, we exhorted him again and again to refrain from confirming the Civil Constitution of the Clergy which would lead the nation into wrong and the kingdom into schism. For by no policy should it be made possible that a political assembly composed of mere men might change the universal discipline of the Church, the teachings of the holy Fathers, abolish the decrees of our Councils, overthrow the hierarchical order, govern the elections of bishops at their own discretion, destroy the sees of our bishops, and, banishing the higher form, impose the baser upon the Church. . . . To be sure the most Christian king refrained from giving the constitution his sanction; but under the insistence and pressure of the National Assembly, he permitted himself to be carried away to the extent of lending his approval thereto. . . . We ourselves . . . subjected all the articles of the aforemen-

[17] Stewart, *op. cit.*, pp. 185-187.

tioned constitution to an examination; but the Assembly
of the French nation, although hearing the united voices
of the Church, was none the less so far from desisting
from the course begun that it tried even more sorely the
resolve of the bishops. Accordingly, seeing this and
being definitely informed by the metropolitans and the
older bishops that no one could be found who would
consider himself capable of confirming the new bishops
elected by laymen, heretics, infidels and Jews in municipal districts as the published decrees provided, and
seeing that the absurd form of this regime could in no
way be maintained, since without bishops all semblance
of a church would vanish, I recalled that even more absurd decrees were published such as those issued on . . .
November 27 [*Document No. 16,* above]. . . . These
very decrees were the reason why the French bishops
. . . took up the fight against the Constitution of the
Clergy. . . . The result of which is that, with the open
avowal and agreement of the entire French Church, the
civil oath is to be regarded as perjured and sacrilegious
. . . and that all committing the act are to be regarded
as schismatic, and as worthless, futile, and subject to
greater censure. . . . Therefore, in order to establish a
barrier to the growing schism at the very first opportunity, to recall the erring to their duties, to maintain
the good in their resolution, we, abiding by the counsel
of our reverend brothers, the cardinals of the Holy
Roman Church, in deference to the prayers of all the
bishops of the French Church and following the prece-
dents established by our predecessors, we, by virtue of
the apostolic power which we exercise, and in view of
the trend of events, declare first that all cardinals of the
Holy Roman Church, . . . archbishops, bishops, abbots,
vicars, canons, parish priests, presbyters and all who are
enlisted in the service of the Church, whether secular or
regular, who have taken the civil oath pure and simple as
prescribed by the National Assembly, which oath is the
poisoned fountainhead and source of all errors and pre-
eminently a cause of mourning to the Catholic Church of
France, shall be suspended from the tenure of any office
whatsoever and liable to the charge of irregularity if they
exercise such office, unless within forty days, dating from
today, they have retracted said oath.

Moreover, we declare specifically that the elections of
. . . Expilly, Marolles, Suarine, Massieu, Lindet, Lau-
rent, Heraudin and Gobel . . . are illegitimate, sacrilegious, and were and are absolutely null and void. . . .

Moreover, in order to anticipate a sequence of greater
evils . . . we decree and declare that all other elections
to French churches . . . were, are, and shall be void,
illegitimate, sacrilegious and absolutely noneffective, and
we rescind, cancel and abrogate them now and forever-
more; declaring in this connection that those falsely and
illegally elected, and others elected in a similar manner,
to churches, either cathedral or parish, are utterly devoid
of spiritual jurisdiction in the governing of souls. . . .

— Document No. 18 —

THE CONCORDAT OF 1801 [18]

The concordat agreed to by Pope Pius VII and the First French Republic, July 15, 1801, follows.

✓   ✓   ✓

The Government of the Republic recognizes that the Catholic, Apostolic and Roman religion is the religion of the vast majority of French citizens.

His Holiness, for his part, recognizes that this same religion has received and is receiving at the present time the greatest benefit and prestige from the establishment of Catholic worship in France and from the individual professions of it which are made by the Consuls of the French Republic.

As a result, after this mutual recognition, they have, for the good of religion and the maintenance of internal peace, agreed on the following:

ARTICLE 1. The Catholic, Apostolic and Roman religion shall be freely practised in France; its worship shall be public, in conformity with police regulations which the Government shall judge to be necessary for public tranquillity.

ARTICLE 2. The Holy See, in conjunction with the Government, shall make a new delimitation of the French dioceses.

ARTICLE 3. His Holiness shall declare to the titular holders of French bishoprics that he expects with firm confidence the utmost sacrifice from them, even if it be that of their Sees, for the sake of peace and unity. After

[18] Ehler and Morrall, *op. cit.*, pp. 252-254.

this exhortation, if they refuse this sacrifice prescribed by the good of the Church (a refusal which, however, His Holiness does not expect), the appointment of new nominees to the government of the bishoprics, according to their new delimitation, shall be proceeded with in the following manner.

ARTICLE 4. The First Consul of the Republic shall, within three months following the publication of a Bull of His Holiness, nominate to archbishoprics and bishoprics, according to the new delimitation. His Holiness shall confer canonical institution, according to the forms established in regard to France before the change of government.

ARTICLE 5. Nominations to bishoprics which shall fall vacant in the future shall also be made by the First Consul and canonical institution shall be given by the Holy See in conformity with the preceding article.

ARTICLE 6. The bishops, before commencing their duties, shall take personally between the hands of the First Consul the oath of fidelity which was in use before the change of government, expressed in the following terms: "I swear and promise to God on the Holy Gospels to observe obedience and fidelity to the Government established by the Constitution of the French Republic. I also promise not to have any knowledge, not to take part in any scheme, not to associate in any conspiracy, whether internal or external, which may be inimical to public tranquillity and, if in my diocese or elsewhere, I learn that something prejudicial to the State is contemplated, I will make it known to the Government."

ARTICLE 7. Ecclesiastics of subordinate rank shall take the same oath between the hands of civil authorities, designated by the Government.

ARTICLE 8. The following form of prayer shall be recited at the end of Divine worship in all the Churches in France: "O Lord, save the Republic. O Lord, save the Consuls."

ARTICLE 9. The bishops shall make a new delimitation of the parishes of their dioceses; this shall not come into effect without the consent of the Government.

ARTICLE 10. The bishops shall nominate parish priests. Their choice shall not fall on any except persons approved by the Government.

ARTICLE 11. The bishops will be able to have a Chapter in their Cathedral, and a seminary for their diocese, but the Government does not guarantee to subsidize them.

ARTICLE 12. All metropolitan churches, cathedrals, parish, churches and others not alienated which are necessary for worship, shall be put at the disposal of the bishops.

ARTICLE 13. His Holiness, for the sake of peace and the happy restoration of the Catholic religion, declares that neither himself nor his successors will disturb in any way those who have acquired alienated Church property and that in consequence the ownership of such property, and the rights and revenues attached to it, shall remain unchallenged in their possession or in that of their heirs.

ARTICLE 14. The Government will guarantee a suitable settlement for bishops and parish priests whose dioceses and livings shall be affected by the new delimitation.

ARTICLE 15. The government will also take measures to ensure that French Catholics can, if they desire, make bequests in favour of churches.

ARTICLE 16. His Holiness recognizes to the First Consul of the French Republic the same rights and prerogatives which the former Government enjoyed in relation to the Holy See.

ARTICLE 17. It is agreed between the contracting parties that in the event that any of the successors of the present First Consul shall not be a Catholic, the rights and prerogatives mentioned in the previous Article and the nomination to bishoprics shall be arranged in collaboration with him by a new convention.

The ratification shall be exchanged at Paris within fourteen days.

— Document No. 19 —

THE DECREES OF THE VATICAN COUNCIL, 1870[19]

Pius IX, at the Vatican Council, formally proclaimed the papal primacy and the dogma of papal infallibility in the First Dogmatic Constitution of the Church of Christ.

✓   ✓   ✓

We therefore teach and declare that, according to the testimony of the Gospel, the primacy of jurisdiction over the universal Church of God was immediately and directly promised and given to blessed Peter the Apostle by Christ the Lord. For it was to Simon alone, to whom He had already said, 'Thou shalt be called Cephas' (*St. John i. 42*), that the Lord, after the confession made by him, saying 'Thou art the Christ, the Son of the living God,' addressed these solemn words: 'Blessed art thou, Simon Bar-Jona, because flesh and blood have not revealed it to thee, but my Father who is in heaven. And I say to thee that thou art Peter, and upon this rock I will build My Church; and the gates of hell shall not prevail against it. And I will give to thee the keys of the kingdom of heaven. And whatsoever thou shalt bind upon earth, it shall be bound also in heaven; and whatsoever thou shalt loose on earth, it shall be loosed in heaven' (*St. Matthew xvi 16-19*) And it was upon Simon alone that Jesus after His resurrection bestowed the jurisdiction of Chief Pastor and Ruler over all His

[19] Monsignor Capel, *A Reply to the Right Hon. W. E. Gladstone's* Political Expostulation, 2nd. ed. (London, 1875) pp. 70-77.

fold in the words: 'Feed My lambs; feed My sheep' (*St. John xxi. 15-17*). At open variance with this clear doctrine of Holy Scripture, as it has been ever understood by the Catholic Church, are the perverse opinions of those who, while they distort the form of government established by Christ the Lord in His Church, deny that Peter in his single person, preferably to all the other Apostles, whether taken separately or together, was endowed by Christ with a true and proper primacy of jurisdiction; or of those who assert that the same primacy was not bestowed immediately and directly upon Blessed Peter himself, but upon the Church, and through the Church on Peter as her minister.

If any one, therefore, shall say that Blessed Peter the Apostle was not appointed the Prince of the Apostles and the visible Head of the whole Church Militant; or that the same directly and immediately received from the same our Lord Jesus Christ a primacy of honour only, and not of true and proper jurisdiction; let him be anathema.

CHAPTER II—ON THE PERPETUITY OF THE PRIMACY
OF BLESSED PETER IN THE ROMAN PONTIFFS

That which the Prince of Shepherds and great Shepherd of the sheep, Jesus Christ our Lord, established in the person of the Blessed Apostle Peter, to secure the perpetual welfare and lasting good of the Church, must, by the same institution, necessarily remain unceasingly in the Church; which, being founded upon the Rock, will stand firm to the end of the world. For none can doubt, and it is known to all ages, that the holy and Blessed Peter, the Prince and Chief of the Apostles, the pillar of the Catholic Church, received the keys of the kingdom from our Lord Jesus Christ, the Saviour and Redeemer of mankind, and lives, presides, and judges, to this day and always, in his successors the Bishops of the Holy See of Rome, which was founded by him, and consecrated by his blood. Whence, whosoever succeeds to Peter in this See does by the institution of Christ Himself obtain the Primacy of Peter over the whole Church. The disposition made by Incarnate Truth therefore remains, and Blessed Peter, abiding in the rock strength which he received has not abandoned the direction of the Church.

Wherefore it has at all times been necessary that every particular Church—that is to say, the faithful throughout the world—should come to the Church of Rome, on account of the greater princedom it has received; so that in this See, whence the rights of venerable communion spread to all, they might, as members joined together in their head, grow closely into one body.

If, then, any shall say that it is not by the institution of Christ the Lord, or by divine right, that Blessed Peter has a perpetual line of successors in the Primacy over the universal Church; or that the Roman Pontiff is not the successor of Blessed Peter in this primacy; let him be anathema.

CHAPTER IV—CONCERNING THE INFALLIBLE TEACHING OF THE ROMAN PONTIFF

. . . Faithfully adhering to the tradition received from the beginning of the Christian faith, for the glory of God our Saviour, the exaltation of the Catholic Religion, and the salvation of Christian people, with the approval of the Sacred Council, We teach and define that it is a dogma divinely revealed: That the Roman Pontiff, when he speaks *ex cathedra,* that is, when in discharge of the office of Pastor and Teacher of all Christians, by virtue of his supreme Apostolic authority, he defines a doctrine regarding faith or morals to be held by the universal Church, is, by the divine assistance promised to him in Blessed Peter, possessed of that infallibility with which the divine Redeemer willed that His Church should be endowed in defining doctrine regarding faith or morals; and that therefore such definitions of the Roman Pontiff are of themselves, and not from the consent of the Church, irreformable.

— Document No. 20 —

POPE LEO XIII'S ENCYCLICAL *IMMORTALE DEI*, 1885 [20]

In 1885 French Catholics were deeply involved in a controversy on the attitude that they should take towards the Third Republic. In his encyclical Immortale Dei *(1885), Leo XIII clarified the Church's position on the problem of Church and State as a guide to Christians living in an age of liberal regimes.*

✓   ✓   ✓

. . . As no society can hold together unless some one be over all, directing all to strive earnestly for the common good, every civilized community must have a ruling authority, and this authority, no less than society itself, has its source in nature, and has, consequently, God for its author. Hence, it follows that all public power must proceed from God. For God alone is the true and supreme Lord of the world. Everything, without exception, must be subject to Him, and must serve Him, so that whosoever holds the right to govern holds it from one sole and single source, namely, God, the sovereign Ruler of all. "There is no power but from God" (*Rom. xiii. 1*).

The right to rule is not necessarily, however, bound up with any special mode of government. It may take this or that form, provided only that it be of a nature to insure the general welfare. But, whatever be the nature of the government, rulers must ever bear in mind that God is the paramount ruler of the world, and must set Him before themselves as their exemplar and law in the administration of the State. For, in things visible God has fashioned secondary causes, in which His divine action can in some wise be discerned, leading up to the end to which the course of the world is ever tending. In like manner, in civil society, God has always willed that there

[20] Courtesy, Catholic Truth Society, London.

should be a ruling authority, and that they who are invested with it should reflect the divine power and providence in some measure over the human race.

They, therefore, who rule should rule with even-handed justice, not as masters, but rather as fathers, for the rule of God over man is most just, and is tempered always with a father's kindness. Government should, moreover, be administered for the well-being of the citizens, because they who govern others possess authority solely for the welfare of the State. . . .

The Almighty, therefore, has given the charge of the human race to two powers, the ecclesiastical and the civil, the one being set over divine, and the other over human, things. (*See Document No. 5.*) Each in its kind is supreme, each has fixed limits, within which it is contained, limits which are defined by the nature and special object of the province of each, so that there is, we may say, an orbit traced out within which the action of each is brought into play by its own native right. But, inasmuch as each of these two powers has authority over the same subjects, and as it might come to pass that one and the same thing—related differently, but still remaining one and the same thing—might belong to the jurisdiction and determination of both, therefore God, who foresees all things, and who is the author of these two powers, has marked out the course of each in right correlation to the other. "For the powers that are, are ordained of God." Were this not so, deplorable contentions and conflicts would often arise, and, not infrequently, men, like travelers at the meeting of two roads, would hesitate in anxiety and doubt, not knowing what course to follow. Two powers would be commanding contrary things, and it would be a dereliction of duty to disobey either of the two.

But it would be most repugnant to them to think thus of the wisdom and goodness of God. Even in physical things, albeit of a lower order, the Almighty has so combined the forces and springs of nature with tempered action and wondrous harmony that no one of them clashes with any other, and all of them most fitly and aptly work together for the great purpose of the universe. There must, accordingly, exist between these two powers a certain orderly connection, which may be compared to the union of the soul and body in man. The nature and scope of that connection can be determined only, as We have laid down, by having regard to the nature of each power, and by taking account of the relative excellence and nobleness of their purpose. One of the two has for its proximate and chief object the well-being of this mortal life; the other, the everlasting joys of heaven. Whatever, therefore, in things human is of a sacred character, whatever belongs either of its own nature or by reason of the end to which it is referred, to the salvation of souls, or to the worship of God, is subject to the power and judgment of the Church. Whatever is to be ranged under the civil and political order is rightly subject to the civil authority. Jesus Christ has Himself given command that what is Caesar's is to be rendered to Caesar, and that what belongs to God is to be rendered to God.

There are, nevertheless, occasions when another method of concord is available for the sake of peace and liberty: We mean when rulers of the State and the Roman Pontiff come to an understanding touching some special matter. At such times the Church gives signal proof of her motherly love by showing the greatest possible kindliness and indulgence. . . .

Sad it is to call to mind how the harmful and lamentable rage for innovation which rose to a climax in the sixteenth century threw first of all into confusion the Christian religion, and next, by natural sequence, invaded the precincts of philosophy, whence it spread amongst all classes of society. From this source, as from a fountain-head, burst forth all those later tenets of unbridled license which, in the midst of the terrible upheavals of the last century, were wildly conceived and boldly proclaimed as the principles and foundation of that new jurisprudence which was not merely previously unknown, but was at variance on many points with not only the Christian, but even the natural law.

Amongst these principles the main one lays down that as all men are alike by race and nature, so in like manner all are equal in the control of their life; that each one is so far his own master as to be in no sense under the rule of any other individual; that each is free to think on every subject just as he may choose, and to do whatever he may like to do; that no man has any right to rule over other men. In a society grounded upon such maxims all government is nothing more nor less than the will of the people, and the people, being under the power of itself alone, is alone its own ruler. It does choose nevertheless, some to whose charge it may commit itself, but in such wise that it makes over to them not the right so much as the business of governing, to be exercised, however, in its name.

The authority of God is passed over in silence, just as if there were no God; or as if he cared nothing for human society; or as if men, whether in their individual capacity or bound together in social relations, owed nothing to God; or as if there could be a government of which the whole origin and power and authority did not reside in God himself. Thus, as is evident, a State becomes nothing but a multitude which is its own master and ruler. And since the people is declared to contain within itself the springhead of all rights and of all power, it follows that the State does not consider itself bound by any kind of duty toward God. . . .

And it is part of this theory that all questions that concern religion are to be referred to private judgment; that every one is to be free to follow whatever religion he prefers, or none at all if he disapproves of all. From this the following consequences logically flow: that the judgment of each one's conscience is independent of all law; that the most unrestrained opinions may be openly expressed as to the practice or omissions of divine worship; and that every one has unbounded license to think whatever he chooses and to publish abroad whatever he thinks. . . .

To hold, therefore, that there is no difference in matters of religion between forms that are unlike each other, and even contrary to each other, most clearly leads in the end to the rejection of all religion in both theory and practice. And this is the same thing as atheism, however it may differ from it in name. Men who really believe in the existence of God must, in order to be consistent with themselves and to avoid absurd conclusions, understand that differing modes of divine worship involving dissimilarity and conflict even on most important points cannot all be equally probable, equally good and equally acceptable to God. . . .

From these pronouncements of the Popes it is evident that the origin of public power is to be sought for in God Himself, and not in the multitude, and that it is repugnant to reason to allow free scope for sedition. Again, that it is not lawful for the State, any more than for the individual, either to disregard all religious duties or to hold in equal favor different kinds of religion; that the unrestrained freedom of thinking and of openly making known one's thoughts is not inherent in the rights of citizens, and is by no means to be reckoned worthy of favor and support. In like manner it is to be understood that the Church no less than the State itself is a society perfect in its own nature and its own right, and that those who exercise sovereignty ought not so to act as to compel the Church to become subservient or subject to them, or to hamper her liberty in the management of her own affairs, or to despoil her in any way of the other privileges conferred upon her by Jesus Christ. In matters, however, of mixed jurisdiction, it is in the highest degree consonant to nature, as also to the designs of God, that so far from one of the powers separating itself from the other, or still less coming into conflict with it, complete harmony, such as is suited to the end for which each power exists, should be preserved between them.

This, then, is the teaching of the Catholic Church concerning the constitution and government of the State. By the words and decrees just cited, if judged dispassionately, no one of the several forms of government is in itself condemned, inasmuch as none of them contains anything contrary to Catholic doctrine, and all of them are capable, if wisely and justly managed, to insure the welfare of the State. Neither is it blameworthy in itself, in any manner, for the people to have a share greater or less, in the government: for at certain times, and under certain laws, such participation may not only be of benefit to the citizens, but may even be of obligation. Nor is there any reason why any one should accuse the Church of being wanting in gentleness of action or largeness of view, or of being opposed to real and lawful liberty. The Church, indeed, deems it unlawful to place the various forms of divine worship on the same footing as the true religion, but does not, on that account, condemn those rulers who, for the sake of securing some great good or of hindering some great evil, allow patiently custom or usage to be a kind of sanction for each kind of religion having its place in the State. And, in fact the Church is wont to take earnest heed that no one shall be forced to embrace the Catholic faith against his will, for, as St. Augustine wisely reminds us, "Man cannot believe otherwise than of his own will."

In the same way the Church cannot approve of that liberty which begets a contempt of the most sacred laws of God, and casts off the obedience due to lawful authority, for this is not liberty so much as license, and is most correctly styled by St. Augustine the "liberty of self-ruin," and by the Apostle St. Peter the "cloak of malice." Indeed, since it is opposed to reason, it is a true slavery, "for whosoever committeth sin is the slave of sin." On the other hand, that liberty is truly genuine, and to be sought after, which in regard to the individual does not allow men to be the slaves of error and of passion, the worst of all masters; which, too, in public administration guides the citizens in wisdom and provides for them increased means of well-being; and which further, protects the State from foreign interference.

This honorable liberty, alone worthy of human beings, the Church approves most highly and has never slackened her endeavor to preserve, strong and unchanged, among nations.

And, in truth, whatever in the State is of chief avail for the common welfare; whatever has been usefully established to curb the license of rulers who are opposed to the true interests of the people, or to keep in check the leading authorities from unwarrantable interfering in municipal or family affairs; whatever tends to uphold the honor, manhood and equal rights of individual citizens —of all these things, as the monuments of past ages bear witness, the Catholic Church has always been the originator, the promoter, or the guardian. Ever, therefore, consistent with herself, while on the one hand she rejects that exorbitant liberty which in individuals and in nations ends in license or in thraldom, on the other hand she willingly and most gladly welcomes whatever improvements the age brings forth, if these really secure the prosperity of life here below, which is, as it were, a stage in the journey to the life that will know no ending.

Therefore, when it is said that the Church is jealous of modern political regimes and that she repudiates the discoveries of modern research, the charge is ridiculous and groundless calumny. Wild opinions she does repudiate, wicked and seditious projects she does condemn, together with that attitude of mind which points to the beginning of a willful departure from God. But, as all truth must necessarily proceed from God, the Church recognizes in all truth that is reached by research a trace of the divine intelligence. And as all truth in the natural order is powerless to destroy belief in the teaching of revelation, but can do much to confirm it, and as every newly discovered truth may serve to further the knowledge or the praise of God, it follows that whatsoever spreads the range of knowledge will always be willingly and even joyfully welcomed by the Church. She will always encourage and promote, as she does in other branches of knowledge, all study occupied with the investigation of nature. In these pursuits, should the human intellect discover anything not known before, the Church makes no opposition. She never objects to search being made for things that minister to the refinements and comforts of life. So far indeed from opposing these she is now, as she ever has been, hostile alone to indolence and sloth, and earnestly wishes that the talents of men may bear more and more abundant fruit by cultivation and exercise. Moreover, she gives encouragement to every kind of art and handicraft, and through her influence, directing all strivings after progress toward virtue and salvation, she labors to prevent man's intellect and industry from turning away from God and heavenly things.

All this, though so reasonable and full of counsel, finds little favor nowadays when States not only refuse to conform to the rules of Christian wisdom, but seem even anxious to recede from them and further on each successive day. Nevertheless, since truth when brought to light is wont, of its own nature, to spread itself far and wide, and gradually take possession of the minds of men, We, moved by the great and holy duty of Our apostolic mission to all nations, speak, as We are bound to do, with freedom. Our eyes are not closed to the spirit of the times. We repudiate not the assured and useful improvements of our age, but devoutly wish affairs of State to take a safer course than they are now taking, and to rest on a more firm foundation without injury to the true freedom of the people; for the best parent and guardian of liberty amongst men is truth. "The truth shall make you free" (*John viii, 32*).

— Document No. 21 —

POPE LEO XIII'S ENCYCLICAL ON LIBERTY: *LIBERTAS HUMANA,* 1888 [21]

In his encyclical on Liberty, *given in 1888, Pope Leo XII defined the stand of the Church on the "modern liberties" which were the source of so much controversy in the nineteenth century.*

✓   ✓   ✓

The nature of human liberty, however it be considered, whether in individuals or in society, whether in those who command or in those who obey, supposes the necessity of obedience to some supreme and eternal law, which is no other than the authority of God, commanding good and forbidding evil. And, so far from this most just authority of God over men diminishing, or even destroying their liberty, it protects and perfects it, for the real perfection of all creatures is found in the prosecution and attainment of their respective ends; but the supreme end to which human liberty must aspire is God. . . .

[21] *Human Liberty: Encyclical Letter of Pope Leo XIII, Libertas Humana* (New York, 1941) pp. 10-24. Courtesy of the Paulist Press.

What Naturalists or Rationalists aim at in philosophy, that the supporters of Liberalism, carrying out the principles laid down by naturalism, are attempting in the domain of morality and politics. The fundamental doctrine of Rationalism is the supremacy of the human reason, which, refusing due submission to the divine and eternal reason proclaims its own independence, and constitutes itself the supreme principle and source and judge of truth. Hence, these followers of Liberalism deny the existence of any divine authority to which obedience is due, and proclaim that every man is the law to himself; from which arises that ethical system which they style independent morality, and which, under the guise of liberty exonerates man from any obedience to the commands of God, and substitutes a boundless license. The end of all this is not difficult to foresee, especially when society is in question. For, when once man is firmly persuaded that he is subject to no one, it follows that the efficient cause of the unity of civil society is not to be sought in any principle external to man, or superior to him, but simply in the free will of individuals; that the authority in the State comes from the people only; and that just as every man's individual reason is his only rule of life, so the collective reason of the community should be the supreme guide in the management of all public affairs. Hence the doctrine of the supremacy of the greatest number, and that all right and all duty reside in the majority. But, from what has been said, it is clear that all this is in contradiction to reason. . . .

We must now consider briefly liberty of speech and liberty of the press. It is hardly necessary to say that there can be no such right as this, if it be not used in moderation, and if it pass beyond the bounds and end of all true liberty. For right is a moral power which it is absurd to suppose that nature has accorded indifferently to truth and falsehood, to justice and injustice. Men have a right freely and prudently to propagate throughout the State what things soever are true and honorable, so that as many as possible may possess them; but lying opinions than which no mental plague is greater, and vices which corrupt the heart and moral life, should be diligently repressed by the public authority, lest they insidiously work the ruin of the State. The excesses of an unbridled intellect, which unfailingly end in the oppression of the untutored multitude, are no less rightly controlled by the authority of the law than are the injuries inflicted by violence upon the weak. And this, all the more surely because by far the greater part of the community is either absolutely unable, or able only with great difficulty, to escape from illusions and deceitful subtleties, especially such as flatter the passions. If unbridled license of speech and of writing be granted to all, nothing will remain sacred and inviolate; even the highest and truest mandates of nature, justly held to be the common and noblest heritage of the human race, will not be spared. Thus, truth being gradually obscured by darkness, pernicious and manifold error, as too often happens, will easily prevail. Thus, too, license will gain what liberty loses; for liberty will ever be more free and secure in proportion as license is kept in fuller restraint. In regard, however, to all matters of opinion which God leaves to man's free discussion, full liberty of thought and of speech is naturally within the right of everyone; for such liberty never leads men to suppress the truth but often to discover it and make it known.

A like judgment must be passed upon what is called liberty of teaching. There can be no doubt that truth alone should imbue the minds of men, for in it are found the well-being, the end and the perfection of every intelligent nature; and therefore nothing but truth should be taught both to the ignorant and to the educated, so as to bring knowledge to those who have it not, and to preserve it in those who possess it. For this reason it is plainly the duty of all who teach to banish error from the mind, and by sure safeguards to close the entry to all false convictions. From this it follows, as is evident, that the liberty of which We have been speaking is greatly opposed to reason, and tends absolutely to pervert men's minds, in as much as it claims for itself the right of teaching whatever it pleases—a liberty which the State cannot grant without failing in its duty. And the more so because the authority of teachers has great weight with their hearers, who can rarely decide for themselves as to the truth or falsehood of the instruction given to them. . . .

Another liberty is widely advocated, namely, liberty of

conscience. If by this is meant that everyone may, as he chooses, worship God or not, it is sufficiently refuted by the arguments already adduced. But it may also be taken to mean that every man in the State may follow the will of God and, from a consciousness of duty and free from every obstacle, obey His commands. This, indeed, is true liberty, a liberty worthy of the sons of God, which nobly maintains the dignity of man and is stronger than all violence or wrong—a liberty which the Church has always desired and held most dear. This is the kind of liberty the Apostles claimed for themselves with intrepid constancy. . . .

Yet with the discernment of a true mother, the Church weighs the great burden of human weakness, and well knows the course down which the minds and actions of men are in this our age being borne. For this reason, while not conceding any right to anything save what is true and honest, she does not forbid public authority to tolerate what is at variance with truth and justice, for the sake of avoiding some greater evil, or of obtaining or preserving some greater good. . . .

And as to tolerance it is surprising how far removed from the equity and prudence of the Church are those who profess what is called liberalism. For, in allowing that boundless license of which we have spoken they exceed all limits, and end at last by making no apparent distinction between truth and error, honesty and dishonesty. And because the Church, the pillar and ground of truth, and the unerring teacher of morals, is forced utterly to reprobate and condemn tolerance of such an abandoned and criminal character, they calumniate her as being wanting in patience and gentleness, and thus fail to see that, in so doing, they impute to her as a fault what is in reality a matter for commendation. But, in spite of all this show of tolerance, it very often happens that, while they profess themselves ready to lavish liberty on all in the greatest profusion, they are utterly intolerant toward the Catholic Church by refusing to allow her the liberty of being herself free.

— Document No. 22 —

POPE LEO XIII'S ENCYCLICAL ON THE CONDITION OF WORKERS, 1891 [22]

Rerum novarum (1894), the most important encyclical of Leo XIII, and one which Pius XI was to call forty years later the Magna Charta of Christian social activity, was a courageous challenge to the economic liberalism and socialism of the nineteenth century. Many of its pleas have become the common practice and policies of governments and peoples in the Western world.

⸸   ⸸   ⸸

The foremost duty, therefore, of the rulers of the State should be to make sure that the laws and institutions, the general character and administration of the commonwealth, shall be such as of themselves to realize public well-being and private prosperity. This is the proper scope of wise statesmanship and the work of the heads of the State. Now a State chiefly prospers and thrives through moral rule, well-regulated family life, respect for religion and justice, the moderation and fair imposing of public taxes, the progress of the arts and of trade, the abundant yield of the land—through everything, in fact, which makes the citizens better and happier. Hereby, then, it lies in the power of a ruler to benefit every class in the State, and amongst the rest to promote to the utmost the interests of the poor; and this in virtue of his office, and without being open to suspicion of undue interference—since it is the province of the State to consult the common good. And the more that is done for the benefit of the working classes by the general laws of the country, the less need will there be for special means to relieve them. . . .

[22] Courtesy, Catholic Truth Society, London.

Whenever the general interest or any particular class suffers, or is threatened with harm, which can in no other way be met, the public authority must step in to deal with it.

Now, it is to the interests of the State, as well as of the individual, that peace and good order should be maintained; that family life should be carried on in accordance with God's laws and those of nature; that Religion should be reverenced and obeyed; that a high standard of morality should prevail, both in public and private life; that justice should be held sacred and that no one should injure another with impunity; that the members of the commonwealth should grow up to man's estate strong and robust, and capable, if need be, of guarding and defending their country. If by a strike, or other combination of workmen, there should be imminent danger of disturbance to the public peace; or if circumstances were such as that among the working class the ties of family life were relaxed; if Religion were found to suffer through the workers not having time and opportunity afforded them to practise its duties; if in workshops and factories there were danger to morals through the mixing of the sexes or from other harmful occasions of evil; or if employers laid burdens upon their workmen which were unjust, or degraded them with conditions repugnant to their dignity as human beings; finally, if health were endangered by excessive labor, or by work unsuited to sex or age—in such cases, there can be no question but that, within certain limits, it would be right to invoke the aid and authority of the law. The limits must be determined by the nature of the occasion which calls for the law's interference—the principle being that the law must not undertake more, nor proceed further, than is required for the remedy of the evil or the removal of the mischief.

Rights must be religiously respected wherever they exist; and it is the duty of the public authority to prevent and to punish injury, and to protect every one in the possession of his own. Still, when there is question of defending the rights of individuals, the poor and badly-off have a claim to especial consideration. The richer class have many ways of shielding themselves, and stand less in need of help from the State; whereas the mass of the poor have no resources of their own to fall back upon, and must chiefly depend upon the assistance of the State. And it is for this reason that wage-earners, since they mostly belong to that class, should be specially cared for and protected by the Government.

Here, however, it is expedient to bring under special notice certain matters of moment. The chief thing is the duty of safeguarding private property by legal enactment and protection. Most of all it is essential, where the passion of greed is so strong, to keep the people within the line of duty; for if all may justly strive to better their condition, neither justice nor the common good allows any individual to seize upon that which belongs to another, or, under the futile and shallow pretext of equality, to lay violent hands on other people's possessions. Most true it is that by far the larger part of the workers prefer to better themselves by honest labor rather than by doing any wrong to others. But there are not a few who are imbued with evil principles and eager for revolutionary change, whose main purpose is to stir up disorder and incite their fellows to acts of violence. The authority of the State should intervene to put restraint upon such firebrands, to save the working classes from being led astray by their manoeuvres, and to protect lawful owners from spoliation.

When work-people have recourse to a strike, it is frequently because the hours of labor are too long, or the work too hard, or because they consider their wages insufficient. The grave inconvenience of this not uncommon occurrence should be obviated by public remedial measures; for such paralysing of labor not only affects the masters and their work-people alike, but is extremely injurious to trade and to the general interests of the public; moreover, on such occasions, violence and disorder are generally not far distant, and thus it frequently happens that the public peace is imperilled. The laws should forestall and prevent such troubles from arising; they should lend their influence and authority to the removal in good time of the causes which lead to conflicts between employers and employed. . . .

If We turn now to things external and material, the first thing of all to secure is to save unfortunate working people from the cruelty of men of greed, who use human beings as mere instruments for money-making. It is neither just nor human so to grind men down with excessive labor as to stupefy their minds and wear out their bodies. . . .

In all agreements between masters and work-people there is always the condition expressed or understood that there should be allowed proper rest for soul and body. To agree in any other sense would be against what is right and just; for it can never be just or right to require on the one side, or to promise on the other, the giving up of those duties which a man owes to his God and to himself.

We now approach a subject of great importance, and one in respect of which, if extremes are to be avoided right notions are absolutely necessary. Wages, as we are told, are regulated by free consent, and therefore the employer, when he pays what was agreed upon, has done his part and seemingly is not called upon to do any thing beyond. The only way, it is said, in which injustice might occur would be if the master refused to pay the whole of the wages, or if the workman should not complete the work undertaken; in such cases the State should intervene, to see that each obtains his due; but not under any other circumstances.

To this kind of argument a fair-minded man will not easily or entirely assent: it is not complete, for there are important considerations which it leaves out of account altogether. To labor is to exert oneself for the sake of procuring what is necessary for the various purposes of life, and chief of all for self-preservation. *In the sweat of thy face thou shalt eat bread* (*Gen. iii, 19*). Hence a man's labor necessarily bears two notes or characters. First of all, it is personal, inasmuch as the force which acts is bound up with the personality and is the exclusive property of him who acts, and, further, was given to him for his advantage. Secondly, man's labor is necessary; for without the result of labor a man cannot live; and self-preservation is a law of nature, which it is wrong to disobey. Now, were we to consider labor merely in so far as it is personal, doubtless it would be within the workman's right to accept any rate of wages whatsoever; for in the same way as he is free to work or not, so is he free to accept a small wage or even none at all. But our conclusion must be very different if together with the personal element in a man's work we consider the fact that work is also necessary for him to live: these two aspects of his work are separable in thought, but not in reality. The preservation of life is the bounden duty of one and all, and to be wanting therein is a crime. It necessarily follows that each one has a natural right to procure what is required in order to live; and the poor can procure that in no other way than by what they can earn through their work.

Let the working man and the employer make free agreements, and in particular let them agree freely as to wages; nevertheless there underlies a dictate of natural justice more imperious and ancient than any bargain between man and man, namely that wages ought not to be insufficient to support a frugal and well behaved wage-carner. If through necessity or fear of a worse evil the workman accepts harder conditions because an employer or contractor will afford him no better, he is made the victim of force and injustice. In these and similar questions however,—such as, for example, the hours of labor in different trades, the sanitary precautions to be observed in factories and workshops, etc.—in order to supersede undue interference on the part of the State, especially as circumstances, times and localities differ so widely, it is advisable that recourse be had to Societies or Boards such as we shall mention presently, or to some other mode of safeguarding the interests of the wage-earners; the State being appealed to, should circumstances require, for its sanction and protection. . . .

Many excellent results will follow from this; and first of all, property will certainly become more equitably divided. For the result of civil change and revolution has been to divide society into two widely differing castes. On the one side there is the party which holds power because it holds wealth; which has in its grasp the whole of labor and trade; which manipulates for its own benefit and its own purposes all the sources of supply, and which is even represented in the councils of the State itself. On the other side there is the needy and powerless multitude, sick and sore in spirit and ever ready for disturbance. If working people can be encouraged to look forward to obtaining a share in the land, the consequence will be

that the gulf between vast wealth and sheer poverty will
be bridged over, and the respective classes will be
brought nearer to one another. A further consequence
will result in the greater abundance of the fruits of the
earth. Men always work harder and more readily when
they work on that which belongs to them; nay, they learn
to love the very soil that yields in response to the labor
of their hands, not only food to eat, but an abundance of
good things for themselves and those dear to them. That
such a spirit of willing labor would add to the produce
of the earth and to the wealth of the community is self-
evident. And a third advantage would spring from this:
men would cling to the country in which they were born;
for no one would exchange his country for a foreign
land if his own afforded him the means of living a decent
and happy life. These three important benefits, however,
can be reckoned on only provided that a man's means be
not drained and exhausted by excessive taxation. The
right to possess private property is derived from nature,
not from man; and the State has the right to control its
use in the interest of the public good alone, but by no
means to absorb it altogether. The State would therefore
be unjust and cruel if under the name of taxation it were
to deprive the private owner of more than is fair. . . .

The most important of all organizations are Working-
men's Unions; for these virtually include all the rest.
History attests what excellent results were brought about
by the Artificers' Guilds of olden times. They were the
means of affording not only many advantages to the
workmen, but in no small degree of promoting the ad-
vancement of art, as numerous monuments remain to
bear witness. Such Unions should be suited to the
requirements of this our age—an age of wider education,
of different habits, and of far more numerous requirements in daily life. It is gratifying to know that there are
actually in existence not a few associations of this nature,
consisting either of workmen alone, or of workmen and
employers together; but it were greatly to be desired that
they should become more numerous and more efficient. . . .

— Document No. 23 —

POPE BENEDICT XV'S PEACE PROPOSALS DURING WORLD WAR I, 1917[23]

In the summer of 1917, Benedict XV, deeming the moment opportune, made his famous peace proposals to the belligerents of World War I. President Wilson, whose position was all important following American entry into the war in April 1917, rejected the proposals on the grounds that the Germans could not be trusted and that negotiations with them would therefore be futile.

↗   ↗   ↗

TO THE HEADS OF THE BELLIGERENT PEOPLES:

From the beginning of our Pontificate, amidst the horrors of the terrible war unleashed upon Europe, We have kept before Our attention three things above all: to preserve complete impartiality in relation to all the belligerents, as is appropriate to him who is the common father and who loves all his children with an equal affection; to endeavor constantly to do all the most possible good, without personal exceptions and without national or religious distinctions, a duty which the universal law of charity, as well as the supreme spiritual charge entrusted to Us by Christ, dictates to Us; finally, as Our peacemaking mission equally demands, to leave nothing undone within Our power, which could assist in hastening the end of this calamity, by trying to lead the peoples and their heads to more moderate frames of mind and to the calm deliberations of peace, of a "just and lasting" peace.

Whoever has followed Our Work during the three unhappy years which have just elapsed, has been able to recognize with ease that We have always remained faithful to Our resolution of absolute impartiality and

[23] Ehler and Morrall, *op. cit.,* pp. 374-377.

to Our practical policy of welldoing. We have never ceased to urge the belligerent peoples and Governments to become brothers once more, even although publicity has not been given to all which We have done to attain this most noble end.

Towards the end of the first year of the war, We addressed to the conflicting nations the most lively exhortations, and in addition We indicated the way to follow in order to arrive at a lasting and honorable peace for all. Unhappily, Our appeal was not heeded. . . . we now wish to descend to more concrete and practical propositions, and to invite the Governments of the belligerent peoples to reach agreement on the following points, which seem to be the basis of a just and lasting peace, leaving to them the task of making them more precise and of completing them.

First of all, the fundamental point should be that for the material force of arms should be substituted the moral force of law; hence a just agreement by all for the simultaneous and reciprocal reduction of armaments, according to rules and guarantees to be established to the degree necessary and sufficient for the maintenance of public order in each State; then, instead of armies, the institution of arbitration, with its lofty peacemaking function, according to the standards to be agreed upon and with sanctions to be decided against the State which might refuse to submit international questions to arbitration or to accept its decisions.

Once the supremacy of law has been established, let every obstacle to the ways of communication between the peoples be removed, by ensuring through rules to be fixed in similar fashion, the true freedom and common use of the seas. This would, on the one hand, remove many reasons for conflict and, on the other, would open new sources of prosperity and progress to all.

With regard to reparations for damage and to the expenses of the war, We see no way of settling the question other than by laying down as a general principle, a complete and reciprocal condonation, justified by the immense benefits to be drawn from disarmament, and all the more because one could not understand the continuation of such slaughter solely for reasons of an economic nature. If, however, in certain cases there exist special reasons, let them be pondered with justice and equity.

But pacifying agreements, with the immense advantages flowing from them, are not possible without reciprocal restitution of territories actually occupied. In consequence, on the part of Germany, there should be total evacuation of Belgium, with a guarantee of its full political, military and economic independence vis-à-vis any Power whatsoever; similarly the evacuation of French territory. On the other side of the other belligerent parties, there should be a corresponding restitution of the German colonies.

With regard to territorial questions, such as those disputed between Italy and Austria, and between Germany and France, there is ground for hope that in consideration of the immense advantages of a lasting peace with disarmament, the conflicting parties will examine them in a conciliatory frame of mind, taking into account so far as it is just and practicable, as We have said previously, the aspirations of the peoples and co-ordinating, according to circumstances, particular interests with the general good of the great human society.

The same spirit of equity and justice should direct the examination of other territorial and political questions, notably those relating to Armenia, the Balkan States and the territories composing the ancient Kingdom of Poland, for which especially its noble historical traditions and the sufferings which it has undergone, particularly during the present war, ought rightly to enlist the sympathies of the nations.

Such are the principal foundations upon which We believe the future reorganization of peoples should rest. They are of a kind which would make impossible the recurrence of such conflicts and would pave the way for a solution of the economic question, so important for the future and the material welfare of all the belligerent States. . . .

— Document No. 24 —

THE LATERAN TREATY AND CONCORDAT BETWEEN THE PAPACY AND ITALY, 1929[24]

The Lateran Treaty of February 11, 1929, settled the Roman Question which had poisoned relations between the papacy and the government of Italy since the seizure of the Papal States in 1870. The Concordat, negotiated at the same time, regulated Church-State relations, while a separate financial convention compensated the papacy in part for the losses it suffered as a result of the seizure of the Papal States. Following the collapse of the Fascist government in World War II, the Lateran Treaty and Concordat were recognized as binding by the 1947 constitution of the Republic of Italy.

✓   ✓   ✓

THE LATERAN TREATY

ARTICLE 1. Italy recognizes and reaffirms the principle contained in Article 1 of the Statute of the Kingdom of March 4, 1848, according to which the Catholic Apostolic and Roman religion is the sole religion of the State.

ARTICLE 2. Italy recognizes the sovereignty of the Holy See in international matters as being an attribute inherent in its nature and in conformity with its tradition and the requirements of its mission in the world.

ARTICLE 3. Italy recognizes the full ownership, absolute power, and sovereign jurisdiction of the Holy See over the Vatican as it is constituted now with all its appurtenances and endowments, thus creating for the special ends and under the conditions stated in the present Treaty the Vatican City. . . .

[24] Ehler and Morrall, *op. cit.*, pp. 385-405.

It is, however, agreed that St. Peter's Square, while being a part of the Vatican City, shall continue to be normally open to the public and subject to the police power of the Italian authorities; this power shall cease to operate at the foot of the steps to the Basilica which continues to be devoted to public worship. The Italian authorities shall, therefore, abstain from ascending the steps and approaching the Basilica unless their intervention is asked for by the competent authority.

Whenever the Holy See may consider it necessary to interrupt temporarily, for some particular purposes, the free traffic of the public in St. Peter's Square, the Italian authorities shall withdraw, unless invited by the competent authority to do otherwise, beyond the external lines of the Bernini colonnade and their prolongation.

ARTICLE 4. The sovereignty and exclusive jurisdiction of the Holy See over the Vatican City, which Italy recognizes, implies that no interference on the part of the Italian government can be exercised in it and that there cannot be any other authority there than that of the Holy See. . . .

ARTICLE 6. Italy shall provide, by means of appropriate agreements with the interested parties, that the Vatican City shall be assured of an adequate water supply of its own. She shall furthermore provide for connection with the State railways by means of a railway station to be constructed in the Vatican City on the spot as indicated on the annexed map and by allowing the railway carriages belonging to the Vatican to circulate on the Italian railways. She shall further provide for direct connection with other States also of telegraphic, telephonic, radio-telegraphic, radio-telephonic and postal services of the Vatican City. . . .

ARTICLE 12. Italy recognizes the right of Legation to the Holy See, active and passive, according to the general rules of International Law. The envoys of the foreign Governments to the Holy See shall continue to enjoy in the Kingdom all prerogatives and immunities appertaining to diplomatic agents under International Law, and their residences may continue to be situated within Italian territory enjoying the immunities due to them according to International Law, even if their States have no diplomatic relations with Italy.

It is understood that Italy engages to leave free always and in every case the correspondence of all States—including belligerent—with the Holy See and vice versa, as well as the access of the bishops of the whole world to the Apostolic See.

The High Contracting Parties undertake to establish normal diplomatic relations between themselves by accrediting an Italian Ambassador to the Holy See and a Papal Nuncio to Italy, who shall be the *doyen* of the Diplomatic Corps in accordance with the customary law recognized by the Congress of Vienna in its Act of June 9, 1815. In consequence of the recognized sovereignty and without prejudice to the provisions of Article 19 below, the diplomats of the Holy See and the couriers sent in the name of the Supreme Pontiff shall enjoy in the territory of the Kingdom, even in time of war, the same treatment as enjoyed by diplomats and diplomatic couriers of other Governments according to the rules of International Law. . . .

ARTICLE 19. The diplomats and envoys of the Holy See, the diplomats and envoys of the foreign governments accredited to the Holy See, and the dignitaries of the Church coming from abroad direct to the Vatican City and provided with passports of the States from which they come, and with due visas of Papal representatives abroad, can proceed without any formalities across the Italian territory to the said City. The same applies to the afore-mentioned persons who, provided with regular Pontifical passports, shall go abroad from the Vatican City. . . .

ARTICLE 21. . . . During the vacancy of the Pontifical See, Italy shall take special precautions that the free transit and access of Cardinals across Italian territory to the Vatican be not hindered, and shall provide that their personal liberty is not impeded or limited.

Italy shall also take measures in her territory surrounding the Vatican City to prevent any acts that may in any way disturb the meetings of the Conclave.

These provisions shall also apply to Conclaves held beyond the boundaries of the Vatican City, and to Councils presided over by the Supreme Pontiff or his Legates, and with regard to bishops summoned to take part in them. . . .

ARTICLE 24. With regard to the sovereignty belonging to it in international matters, the Holy See declares that it remains and shall remain outside all temporal rivalries between other States and shall take no part in international congresses summoned to settle such matters, unless the parties in dispute make jointly appeal to its mission of peace; in any case the Holy See reserves the right of exercising its moral and spiritual power.

Consequently, the Vatican City shall always and in any event be considered as neutral and inviolable territory. . . .

ARTICLE 26. The Holy See considers that in the agreements signed today an adequate guarantee is given providing it with the requisite liberty and independence for the pastoral government of the Roman diocese, and of the Catholic Church in Italy and throughout the world; it declares the "Roman Question" finally and irrevocably settled and hence eliminated, and recognizes the Kingdom of Italy under the Dynasty of the House of Savoy with Rome as the capital of the Italian State.

Italy, on her part, recognizes the State of the Vatican City under the sovereignty of the Supreme Pontiff.

The law of May 13, 1871, no. 214 and any other provisions contrary to the present Treaty are hereby abrogated.

THE CONCORDAT

ARTICLE 1. In the sense of Article 1 of the Treaty [see above, p. 152], Italy assures to the Catholic Church the free exercise of spiritual power, the free and public exercise of worship, and of jurisdiction in ecclesiastical matters in accordance with the provisions of the present Concordat and, if necessary, shall grant to the ecclesiastics protection, through her authorities, with regard to the acts of their spiritual ministry.

In consideration of the sacred character of the Eternal City which is the episcopal See of the Supreme Pontiff, the center of the Catholic world and a place of pilgrimage, the Italian government will take care to keep Rome free from anything which would be inconsistent with such character.

ARTICLE 2. The Holy See shall communicate and correspond freely with the bishops, with the clergy and with the whole Catholic world, without any interference on the part of the Italian government. Similarly, the bishops shall communicate and correspond freely with their clergy and with all the faithful in matters concerning their pastoral ministry. . . .

ARTICLE 16. The High Contracting Parties shall proceed jointly, by means of mixed Commissions, with the revision of the geographical delimitation of the Dioceses for the purpose of making it, so far as possible, correspond to that of the provinces. . . .

ARTICLE 19. The choice of archbishops and bishops belong to the Holy See.

Before proceeding to the nomination of an Archbishop, a diocesan bishop or a coadjutor *cum iure successionis,* the Holy See shall communicate the name of the person chosen to the Italian Government in order to make sure that the Government has no objection of a political nature to the nomination.

The steps necessary in this connection shall be effected with the greatest possible care and with all discretion, so that the name of the person chosen shall remain secret until his actual nomination. . . .

ARTICLE 21. Provision to ecclesiastical benefices belongs to the ecclesiastical authorities. . . .

ARTICLE 25. The Italian State renounces the sovereign prerogative of the Royal Patronage over benefices both major and minor.

Likewise it renounces *la regalia* [i.e. the Crown's right to appropriate to itself the income of benefices during their vacancies] over major and minor benefices. . . .

ARTICLE 28. In order to ease consciences the Holy See grants full pardon to all those who are—in consequence of the Italian laws concerning the patrimony of the Church—in possession of ecclesiastical property.

ARTICLE 29. The Italian State shall revise its legislation in so far as it concerns ecclesiastical matters, reforming and completing it in order to bring it into harmony with the principles which inspired the Treaty concluded with the Holy See and the present Concordat. . . .

ARTICLE 33. The disposal of the catacombs situated at Rome and in other parts of the Kingdom's territory is reserved to the Holy See, with the corresponding duty of keeping them in custody, maintaining and conserving them. Consequently the Holy See can, while observing the laws of the State and saving the possible rights of third parties, proceed to any suitable excavations and to the transfer of sacred remains.

ARTICLE 34. Wishing to restore to the institution of matrimony, which is the foundation of the family, the dignity conformable to the Catholic tradition of its people, the Italian State recognizes the civil effect of the Sacrament of Matrimony as regulated by Canon Law. . . .

ARTICLE 36. Italy considers the teaching of Christian doctrine in the form shaped by Catholic tradition as the basis and goal of public education. She, therefore, agrees that the teaching of religion, which is now given in the public elementary schools, be in the future extended to and developed in secondary schools, according to a programme to be established by agreement between the Holy See and the State.

This teaching shall be imparted through the medium of teachers and professors who are priests or members of religious Orders approved by ecclesiastical authorities and, in an auxiliary manner, by lay teachers and professors who shall for that purpose be provided with a certificate of qualification, issued by the Ordinary of the diocese in question. .

ARTICLE 39. The Universities, greater or lesser seminaries, diocesan, inter-diocesan or regional, Academies, Colleges and other Catholic institutions for training and education of ecclesiastics, shall continue to depend solely on the Holy See, without any interference on the part of the educational authorities of the Kingdom. . . .

ARTICLE 43. The Italian State recognizes the organizations connected with the Italian "Catholic Action" in so far as these shall—according to the instructions of the Holy See—carry out their activities outside any political party, and under the immediate guidance of the Church's hierarchy for the diffusion and practical application of Catholic principles.

The Holy See avails itself of the opportunity afforded by this provision of the present Concordat to renew the prohibition for all ecclesiastics and religious in Italy, of joining, or working in, any political party.

— Document No. 25 —

POPE PIUS XI'S CONDEMNATION OF FASCISM: *NON ABBIAMO BISOGNO*, 1931 [25]

The conflict between the Church and Fascism, following the signing of the Concordat of 1929, centered around the question of education; Fascist youth organizations claimed a monopoly of education over the younger generations. In his encyclical Non abbiamo bisogno *(1931), Pius XI strongly condemned the Fascist concept of education and of the State.*

✦　　　✦　　　✦

And here We find Ourselves in the presence of a contract between authentic affirmations on the one hand and not less authentic facts on the other hand, which reveal, without the slightest possibility of doubt, the proposal, already in great part actually put into effect, to monopolize completely the young, from the tenderest years up to manhood and womanhood, and all for the exclusive advantage of a party, of a regime based on an ideology which clearly resolves itself into a true and real pagan worship of the state, which is no less in contrast with the natural rights of the family than it is in contradiction to the supernatural rights of the Church. To propose and promote such a monopoly, to persecute for this reason Catholic Action as has been done for some time more or less openly or under cover, to reach this end by striking Catholic Action in the way that has recently occurred, is truly and actually to prevent children from going to Jesus Christ, since it impedes them from going to His Church and even arrives at the point of snatching them with violence from the bosom of both, because where the Church is, there is Jesus Christ.

[25] Courtesy, National Catholic Welfare Conference, Washington, D.C.

The Church of Jesus Christ has never contested the rights and the duties of the state concerning the education of its citizens and We Ourselves have recalled and proclaimed them in Our recent Encyclical Letter on the Christian Education of Youth; rights and duties which are unchallengeable as long as they remain within the limits of the state's proper competency, a competency which in its turn is clearly indicated and determined by the missions of the state, missions certainly not only bodily and material, but missions that by the very necessity of their character are contained within the limits of the natural, the earthly and the temporary.

The universal divine mandate with which the Church of Jesus Christ has been by Jesus Christ Himself incommunicably and absolutely commissioned to concern herself with eternity, with heaven and with the supernatural —with that order of things which on the one side, it is of the strictest obligation for every rational creature to consider and to which, on the other side, it is necessary by the very nature of things to subordinate and co-ordinate the remainder.

The Church of Jesus Christ is certainly acting within the limits of its mandate, not only when it puts into souls the first indispensable beginnings and elements of supernatural life, but also when it assists and encourages the growth of this supernatural life according to the opportunities and the capacities of persons and in the ways and by the means which, in the Church's judgment, seem suitable also with the purpose of preparing capable and efficient collaborators with the apostolic Hierarchy and clergy. It is Jesus Christ Himself Who made the solemn declaration that He came precisely that souls might have not only some beginning or some element of supernatural life, but that they may have it in greater abundance. "I am come that they may have life, and may have it more abundantly" (*John x. 10*).

It was Jesus Christ Himself who laid the foundations of Catholic Action. It was Christ Himself Who, choosing and educating the Apostles and Disciples as collaborators in His Divine Apostolate, gave an example which at once was followed by the first Holy Apostles, as the Sacred Text itself substantiates.

It is, consequently, an unjustified pretense and, indeed,

irreconcilable with the name and the profession of being a Catholic, to come to teach the Church and its Head what is sufficient and what must be sufficient for the education and Christian formation of souls and to enunciate and promote in society, chiefly for the young, the principles of faith and of their full efficiency in life. To the unjustifiable presumption must be added also very clear evidence of the absolute incompetence and complete ignorance of the matters under discussion. Recent events must have opened the eyes of all, since they have demonstrated with evidence that which has come to pass within a few years, not in fact saving, but rather disrupting and destroying the true religious sentiment of Christian and civil education.

A conception of the State which makes the rising generations belong to it entirely, without any exception, from the tenderest years up to adult life, cannot be reconciled by a Catholic either with Catholic doctrine or with the natural rights of the family. It is not possible for a Catholic to accept the claim that the Church and the Pope must limit themselves to the external practices of religion (such as the Mass and the Sacraments), and that all the rest of education belongs to the State.

The erroneous and false doctrines and maxims that We have, up to the present, already pointed out and deplored occurred many times during these last few years, and, as is well known, We have never, with God's help, done any less than Our Apostolic duty in indicating and answering them with the just claims of the genuine Catholic doctrine and with the enunciation of the inviolable rights of the Church of Jesus Christ and of the souls redeemed by His precious blood.

— Document No. 26 —

THE ENCYCLICAL OF POPE PIUS XI ON ATHEISTIC COMMUNISM, 1937[26]

The world-wide depression which began late in 1929 and lasted until the outbreak of World War II, seriously undermined the faith of millions of people in liberal capitalism. Many intellectuals, workers and others were seriously influenced by the apparent social justice involved in the Communist myth of a godless earthly paradise. Pius XI, in his encyclical on Atheistic Communism *(Divini Redemptoris), the first of three major papal utterances in 1937 on totalitarianism, exposed again the essential errors of Communism.*

✓   ✓   ✓

No sooner had the "intellectuals" begun to claim it as their mission to deliver civilization from the shackles of religion and moral control, than Our Predecessors, mindful of their duty, warned the world in plain terms what would be the outcome of thus divorcing human society from Christian principles. And as for communism, its false doctrines were solemnly denounced as long ago as 1846 by Our Predecessor Pius IX, who subsequently included his condemnation in the Syllabus. He wrote, in his Encyclical *Qui pluribus,* of "that infamous doctrine of communism, utterly opposed to the natural law itself, the adoption of which would completely destroy all men's rights, their property and fortune, and even human society itself."

At a later time another of Our Predecessors, Leo XIII, spoke clearly and significantly when he described these same aberrations as "a deadly plague insidiously penetrating the very vitals of human society and threatening

[26] Courtesy, Catholic Truth Society, London.

it with extinction"; and it was with an intuitive power characteristic of his mind that he showed how the organized tendency of the masses toward atheism, occurring in an age of great techinal progress, was the result of a philosophy which had long sought to set up a barrier between science and faith, and between human life and the Church.

We too, more than once during Our Pontificate, have urgently and anxiously called attention to the menacing spread of this tide of wickedness. In 1924, on the return of Our relief mission from Russia, We denounced the false doctrines and methods of communism in a special Address to the whole world; in one Encyclical after another We have solemnly protested against the persecution of Christians in Russia, in Mexico and in Spain; and Our pronouncements last year, on the occasion of the World Exhibition of the Catholic Press, in the audiences granted by Us to Spanish refugees, and in Our broadcast Message on Christmas Eve, are still fresh in the memory.

Indeed, this is the reason why the leaders of this campaign against Christian civilization in Moscow are so unremitting in their attacks upon the Papacy; these bitter enemies of the Church are thus testifying, by their deeds if not by their words, that the papacy is maintaining its tradition of defending the truth of the Christian religion with the faith inviolate, and that the Holy See, of all public authorities on earth, has been most insistent and most emphatic in denouncing and condemning the great peril of communism. . . .

The communism of today, even more pretentiously than similar theories in the past, poses as the savior of the poor. A pseudo-ideal of justice, equality and brotherhood among workers inspires the whole of its theory and practice, permeating the movement with a counterfeit mysticism which, combined with the glamor of illusive promises, both dupes the masses and fills them with a contagious and vehement enthusiasm. And there is no doubt that the movement is assisted by the present situation, in which an unjust distribution of wealth has resulted in widespread and exceptional poverty. Indeed it is the boast of the communists that their ideal has effected an improvement in economic conditions. The truth, however, is that any increase there has been in production is due to other causes: to the intensification of manufacturing industries in countries hitherto devoid of them; to the very profitable exploitation of immense natural resources by brutal methods; and to a harsh system of forced labor by which low wages are paid for extremely heavy work.

The doctrine of modern communism, though sometimes presented in specious attractive guise, is really based upon Marx's theory of dialectical and historical materialism, of which the bolshevist intellectuals claim alone to possess the genuine interpretation. The theory teaches that matter, with its blind and hidden forces, is the only reality which exist, and that it is matter which by a natural process evolves into a tree, an animal, or a man. Even human society is only a particular manifestation or form of matter, evolving in the same way and tending by an irresistible necessity and by a perpetual conflict of forces to the attainment of its final goal, which is a classless society. Such a doctrine obviously leaves no room for the idea of an eternal God, for a distinction between spirit and matter or between body and soul, for the survival of the soul after death, or for any hope of a future life.

Developing the "dialectical" side of their materialism, the communists maintain that the pace of the aforesaid conflict, which is to bring all things to their final consummation, can be accelerated by the action of man. They therefore make it their aim to accentuate the differences between class and class in the community; to represent class warfare, actually the source of so much strife and bloodshed, as a crusade of human progress; and therefore to crush utterly any opposition raised to their systematic violence as though it were a crime against the human race.

The communistic theory, moreover, denies the freedom of man; it deprives him of that which is the principle of his life as a rational being, and so strips the human person of his dignity and of all moral control over his vicious inclinations. And because, for the communists, the human person is nothing more than a cog in the machinery of the world system, they deny to individuals all the natural rights which derive from personality and ascribe them to the community.

In relation to one another all citizens are held to be absolutely equal, and accordingly any divinely constituted authority or subordination of one person to another, even parental authority is repudiated; such power, such subjection as the communists acknowledge, is derived from the State as its first and only source. Nor is any individual allowed the right of ownership over natural resources or the means of production, because, these being the potential source of further wealth, their ownership must necessarily result in some men obtaining power over others. This is why they want to abolish this right of private property altogether, for they hold it to be the chief cause of economic enslavement. . . .

What does human society become, based on these materialistic principles? An association of human beings, with no other principle of unity save an authority deriving from economic factors. Its sole function is to produce wealth by communal labor; and its sole aim is the enjoyment of material goods in a paradise where each man "gives labor according to his strength and receives wealth according to his needs."

It is to be noted also that this system grants the community the right, indeed the practically unlimited and arbitrary power, to direct individual citizens into communal industry regardless of their personal welfare, and even to constrain the unwilling by force. The only moral code, the only law acknowledged in this society, is that which has its origin in the economic system of the time; earthly in origin, therefore, and subject to constant change. Briefly, the object is to introduce a new order and a new civilization, evolved from the hidden forces of nature, and culminating in a godless human society.

When all men have finally acquired the qualities and habitual outlook needed for the formation of such a community and when the classless utopia has at last become a reality, then the political State, whose only purpose at present is to enable capitalists to oppress the proletariat, will in the natural course of things perish and be "liquidated." Meanwhile, and until that happy condition of life is achieved, the communists make use of the government and its authority as being the most effective means available for the attainment of their purpose.

Such, venerable brethren, is the doctrine which bolshevists and atheistic communism preaches to the world as a new gospel, as the harbinger of salvation and deliverance: a doctrine full of error and sophistry, contrary to revelation and reason alike; a doctrine destructive of the foundations of civil society and subversive of social order; a doctrine which refuses to acknowledge the true origin of the State, its true nature and purpose; which repudiates and denies the rights, dignity and the freedom of the human person.

— Document No. 27 —

POPE PIUS XII URGES UNITY IN OPPOSING WORLD EVILS: *SUMMI PONTIFICATUS*, 1939 [27]

On October 20, 1939, six weeks after the outbreak of World War II, Pope Pius XII issued his first encyclical. The blitzkrieg against Poland had just proved to the world the efficiency of the Nazi war machine and foreshadowed the even greater horrors to come. The Pope, whose efforts to avert the war had failed, examines the errors which had led Western civilization to the abyss, appeals again for a return to sanity, for the need of government by law and a return to the teachings of Christ.

✓   ✓   ✓

Among the many errors which flow from the poisoned source of religious and moral agnosticism, We should draw your attention to two in particular, as being those which more than others render almost impossible, or at

[27] Harry C. Koenig, *Principles for Peace: Selections from Papal Documents, Leo XIII to Pius XII* (Washington, 1943). By permission, National Catholic Welfare Conference, Washington, D.C.

least precarious and uncertain, the peaceful intercourse of peoples.

The first of these pernicious errors, widespread today, is the forgetfulness of that law of human solidarity and charity which is dictated and imposed by our common origin and by the equality of rational nature in all men, no matter to what people they belong, and by the redeeming Sacrifice offered by Jesus Christ on the Altar of the Cross to His Heavenly Father on behalf of sinful mankind. . . .

But there is yet another error no less pernicious to the well-being of the nations and to the prosperity of that great human society which gathers together and embraces within its confines all races. It is the error contained in those ideas which do not hesitate to divorce civil authority from every kind of dependence upon the Supreme Being—First Cause and Absolute Master of man and of society—and from every restraint of a Higher Law derived from God as from its First Source. Thus, they accord the civil authority an unrestricted field of action that is at the mercy of the changeful tide of human will, or of the dictates of casual historical claims and of the interests of a few.

Once the authority of God and the sway of His Law are denied in this way, the civil authority as an inevitable result tends to attribute to itself that absolute autonomy which belongs exclusively to the Supreme Maker. It puts itself in the place of the Almighty and elevates the State or group into the last end of life, the supreme criterion of the moral and juridical order, and, therefore, forbids every appeal to the principles of natural reason and of the Christian conscience. We do not, of course, fail to recognize that, fortunately, false principles do not always exercise their full influence, especially when age-old Christian traditions, on which the peoples have been nurtured, remain still deeply, even if unconsciously, rooted in their hearts.

Nonetheless, one must not forget that the essential insufficiency and weakness of every principle of social life which rests upon a purely human foundation, is inspired by merely earthly motives, and relies for its force on the sanction of a purely external authority. Where the dependence of human right upon the divine is denied, where appeal is made only to some insecure idea of a merely human authority, and where an autonomy is claimed which rests only upon a utilitarian morality, there human law itself justly forfeits in its more weighty application the moral force which is the essential condition for its acknowledgement and also for its demand of sacrifices.

It is quite true that power, based on such weak and unsteady foundations, can attain at times, under such chance circumstances, material successes apt to arouse wonder in superficial observers. But the moment comes when the inevitable law triumphs, which strikes down all that has been constructed upon a hidden or open disproportion between the greatness of the material and outward success, and the weakness of the inward value and of its moral foundation. Such disproportion exists whenever public authority disregards or denies the dominion of the Supreme Lawgiver, Who, as He has given rulers power, has also set and marked its bounds. . . .

To consider the State as something ultimate to which everything else should be subordinated and directed, cannot fail to harm the true and lasting prosperity of nations. This can happen either when unrestricted dominion comes to be conferred on the State as having a mandate from the nation, people, or even a social class, or when the State arrogates such dominion to itself as absolute master, despotically, without any mandate whatsoever. If, in fact, the State lays claim to and directs private enterprises, these, ruled as they are by delicate and complicated internal principles which guarantee and assure the realization of their special aims, may be damaged to the detriment of the public good, by being wrenched from their natural surroundings, that is, from responsible private action. . . .

The idea which credits the State with unlimited authority is not simply an error harmful to the internal life of nations, to their prosperity, and to the larger and well ordered increase in their well-being, but likewise it injures the relations between peoples, for it breaks the unity of supranational society, robs the law of nations of its foundation and vigor, leads to violation of others' rights and impedes agreement and peaceful intercourse. A disposition, in fact, of the divinely-sanctioned natural order divides the human race into social groups, nations or States, which are mutually independent in organization and in the direction of their internal life. But for all that, the human race is bound together by reciprocal ties, moral and juridical, into a great commonwealth directed to the good of all nations and ruled by special laws which protect its unity and promote its prosperity. Now no one can fail to see how the claim to absolute autonomy for the State stands in open opposition to this natural law that is inherent in man—nay, denies it utterly—and, therefore, leaves the stability of international relations at the mercy of the will of rulers, while it destroys the possibility of true union and fruitful collaboration directed to the general good.

So, Venerable Brethren, it is indispensable for the existence of harmonious and lasting contacts and of fruitful relations, that the peoples recognize and observe these principles of international natural law which regulate their normal development and activity. Such principles demand respect for corresponding rights to independence, to life and to the possibility of continuous development in the paths of civilization; they demand, further, fidelity to compacts agreed upon and sanctioned in conformity with the principles of the law of nations.

The indispensable presupposition, without doubt, of all peaceful intercourse between nations, and the very soul of the juridical relations in force among them, is mutual trust: the expectation and conviction that each party will respect its plighted word; the certainty that both sides are convinced that *Better is wisdom than weapons of war* (*Eccl. 9.18*), and are ready to enter into discussion and to avoid recourse to force or to threats of force in case of delays, hindrances, changes or disputes, because all these things can be the result not of bad-will, but of changed circumstances and of genuine interests in conflict. But, on the other hand, to tear the law of nations from its anchor in divine law, to base it on the autonomous will of States, is to dethrone that very law and deprive it of its noblest and strongest qualities. Thus it would stand abandoned to the fatal drive of private interest and collective selfishness exclusively intent on the assertion of its own rights and ignoring those of others. . . .

Once the bitterness and cruel strifes of the present have ceased, the new order of the world, of national and international life, must rest no longer on the quicksands of changeable and ephemeral standards that depend only on the selfish interests of groups and individuals. No, they must rest on the unshakable foundation, on the solid rock of natural law and of Divine Revelation. There the human legislator must attain to that balance, that keen sense of moral responsibility, without which it is easy to mistake the boundary between the legitimate use and the abuse of power. Thus only will his decisions have internal consistency, noble dignity and religious sanction, and be immune from selfishness and passion.

For true though it is that the evils from which mankind suffers today come in part from economic instability and from the struggle of interests regarding a more equal distribution of the goods which God has given man as a means of sustenance and progress, it is not less true that their root is deeper and more intrinsic, belonging to the sphere of religious belief and moral convictions which have been perverted by the progressive alienation of the peoples from that unity of doctrine, faith, customs and morals which once was promoted by the tireless and beneficent work of the Church. If it is to have any effect, the reeducation of mankind must be, above all things, spiritual and religious. Hence, it must proceed from Christ as from its indispensable foundation; must be actuated by justice and crowned by charity. . . .

The hour when this Our first Encyclical reaches you is in many respects a real "Hour of Darkness" in which the spirit of violence and discord brings indescribable suffering on mankind. Do We need to give assurance that Our paternal heart is close to all Our children in compassionate love, and especially to the afflicted, the oppressed, the persecuted? The nations swept into the tragic whirlpool of war are perhaps as yet only at the "beginnings of sorrows" (*Mt. 24.8*), but even now there reigns in thousands of families death and desolation, lamentation and misery. The blood of countless human beings, even noncombatants, raises a piteous dirge over a nation such as Our dear Poland, which, for its fidelity to the Church, for its services in the defense of Christian civilization, written in indelible characters in the annals of history, has a right to the generous and brotherly sympathy of the whole world, while it awaits, relying on the powerful intercession of Mary, Help of Christians, the hour of resurrection in harmony with the principles of justice and true peace.

What has already happened and is still happening was presented, as it were, in a vision before Our eyes when, while still some hope was left, We left nothing undone in the form suggested to Us by Our Apostolic office and by the means at Our disposal, to prevent recourse to arms and to keep open the way to an understanding honorable to both parties. Convinced that the use of force on one side would be answered by recourse to arms on the other, We considered it a duty inseparable from Our Apostolic office and of Christian charity to try every means to spare mankind and Christianity the horrors of a world conflagration, even at the risk of having Our intentions and Our aims misunderstood. Our advice, if heard with respect, was not, however, followed and while Our pastoral heart looks on with sorrow and foreboding, the Image of the Good Shepherd comes up before Our gaze, and it seems as though We ought to repeat to the world in His name: *If thou . . . hadst . . . known . . . the things that are to thy peace; but now they are hidden from thy eyes"* (*Luke 19.42*).

— Document No. 28 —

THE PEACE PLAN OF
PIUS XII, 1939 [28]

*In his Christmas message of 1939, Pius XII laid down
the following five point plan for peace.*

FIRST. The fundamental condition of a just and lasting
peace is to assure the right to life and independence of
all nations, large, small, strong or weak. One nation's will
to live must never be tantamount to a death sentence for
another. When this equality of rights has been destroyed,
injured or imperiled, juridical order requires reparation
whose measure and extent are not determined by the
sword or selfish, arbitrary judgment, but by the standards
of justice and reciprocal equity.

SECOND. That order, reestablished in such a manner,
may be tranquil and durable—the cardinal principle of
true peace—nations must be liberated from the heavy
slavery of armaments and the danger that material force,
instead of serving to protect rights, become the tyrannical
violator of them.

Conclusions of peace which failed to attribute fundamental importance to disarmament, mutually accepted,
organic and progressive both in letter and spirit, and
failed to carry out this disarmament loyally, would
sooner or later reveal their inconsistency and lack of
vitality.

THIRD. Any reorganization of international neighbor-
liness should conform with the maximum of human wisdom for all parties concerned to remove the consequences
of past lapses or deficiencies. And, in creating or reconstructing international institutions which have a mission
so high but at the same time difficult and full of serious

[28] Reprinted with permission from *The Catholic Mind*, Vol. 38
(1940) pp. 4-7.

responsibilities, account should be taken of experiences which arose from the inefficacy or defective functioning of similar previous projects.

And, since it is so difficult—one would be tempted to say almost impossible—for human weakness to foresee everything and assure everything at the time of drafting of peace treaties—when it is difficult to be entirely free from passions and bitterness—the establishment of juridical institutions which would serve to guarantee the loyal and faithful carrying out of terms and, in case of recognized need, the revising and correcting of them, is of decisive importance for honorable acceptance of a peace treaty and to avoid arbitrary unilateral ruptures and interpretations of treaty terms.

FOURTH. A point which should be given particular attention if better arrangement of Europe is sought, concerns the real needs and just demands of nations and peoples as well as of ethnical minorities; demands which, if not always sufficient to form a strict right when there are recognized or confirmed treaties or other juridical documents which oppose them, deserve at all events benevolent examination to meet them in a peaceful way and, where it appears necessary, by means of equitable, wise and unanimous revision of treaties.

Once true equilibrium among nations is thus brought back and the basis of mutual trust is reestablished, many of the incentives to resort to violence would be removed.

FIFTH. But even better and more complete settlements will be imperfect and condemned to ultimate failure, if those who guide the destinies of peoples, and the people themselves, refuse to permit themselves to be penetrated ever more by that spirit which alone can give living authority and obligation to the dead letter of articles in international agreements—by that spirit, namely, of intimate, acute responsibility that measures and weighs human statutes according to the holy, unshakable rules of Divine Law; by that hunger and thirst for justice which is proclaimed in the Beatitudes in the Sermon on the Mount, and which has, as a natural presupposition, moral justice; by that universal love which is the compendium and most comprehensive term or Christian ideal, and therefore offers a way also for those who have not the benefit of participating in our own Faith.

We do not fail to recognize the grave difficulties which interpose themselves against the accomplishment of the aims which We have outlined in a desire to lay foundations for, to put into effect and to preserve, a just international peace.

But if ever there were an aim worthy of the concourse of noble, generous spirits; if ever there arose a spiritual crusade which with new truth sounded the cry, "God wills it," it is truly that high aim and this crusade —to lead peoples back from the muddy gulf of material and selfish interest to the living fountain of Divine Law, which alone is powerful and gives that morality, nobility and stability of which a lack has been felt far too long, and which is gravely needed to repair the damage done to most nations, to humanity and to those ideals which are at the same time the real ends of peace based on justice and love.

— Document No. 29 —

POPE PIUS XII'S VIEWS ON THE POWERS OF CHURCH AND STATE, 1945 [29]

*Following the upheavals of World War II, Pius XII ex-
pressed his views on the spiritual power of the Church
and on modern concepts of the State in an allocution to
the Roman Rota at the opening of this tribunal's juridical
year (October 2, 1945).*

It is undeniable that one of the vital exigencies of any
human community, consequently also of the Church and
the State, consists in the permanent assurance of unity
in the diversity of their members.

"Totalitarianism," however, can certainly not satisfy
this exigency because it allows the State power to assume
an undue extension, and to determinate, and to fix, both
in substance and in form, every field of activity, so that
it compresses all legitimate manifestation of life—personal, local, professional—into a mechanical unity or
collectivity under the stamp of nation, race, or class. . . .

However, the above-mentioned fundamental exigency
is also far from being satisfied by that other concept of
civil authority, which may be called "authoritarianism,"
for the latter excludes the citizens from all effective participation in, or influence upon the formation of the will
of the society. Consequently, it splits the nation into two
categories, the rulers and the ruled, and the mutual relationship between the two either becomes purely mechanical, being governed by force, or has no more than a
biological basis.

Who, therefore, would not realize that in this manner
the very nature of State power is completely perverted?

[29] Ehler and Morrall, *op cit.*, pp. 602-607.

The truth is that State power should tend, both in itself and through the exercise of its functions, to make the State a true community, intimately united in a final purpose which is the common good. In the said system, however, the notion of the common good becomes so unstable and appears so obviously as a misleading mask for the unilateral interests of the rulers that a frantic legislative "dynamism" excludes all juridical security and so destroys a basic element of every true judicial order.

Such a false dynamism can never submerge and suppress the essential rights recognized in the Church to the individual persons, both physical and juridical. The nature of ecclesiastical authority has nothing in common with this authoritarianism"; the latter can, therefore, claim no point of resemblance to the hierarchical constitution of the Church.

It remains to examine the democratic forms of government, in which some would like to find a closer similitude to the power of the Church. Undoubtedly, wherever true democracy exists in theory and practice, it satisfies that vital requirement of every sound community to which we have referred. . . . However, the same applies, or could apply, under the same conditions also to other legitimate forms of government.

Certainly the Christian Middle Ages, which were particularly imbued with the spirit of the Church, proved by the abundance of their flourishing democratic communities not only that the Christian faith is able to produce a genuine and true democracy but also that it is the only durable foundation for democracy. A democracy without an accord of spirits, at least as to the fundamental maxims of life—and above all, as to the rights of God, the dignity of the human person and the respect due to the honest activity and liberty of the person—would be defective and unsound even in its political aspect. If, therefore, the people depart from the Christian faith or do not hold it resolutely as the principle of civil life, even democracy is easily altered and deformed, and in the course of time is liable to fall into a one-party "totalitarianism" or "authoritarianism."

On the other hand, if we keep in mind the favorite thesis of democracy—which has been expounded in all ages by outstanding Christian thinkers—namely that the original subject of civil power derived from God is the people (not the "masses"), then the distinction between the Church and even the democratic State becomes increasingly clear.

The ecclesiastical power is, indeed, essentially different from the civil power, and hence its juridical power is also different from that of the State.

The origin of the Church, unlike the origin of the State, is not to be found in Natural Law. The most complete and accurate analysis of the human person offers no ground for the conclusion that the Church, like civil society, was naturally bound to come into existence and to develop. Its existence is derived from a positive act of God beyond and above the social nature of man, though in perfect accord with it; therefore, the ecclesiastical power—and consequently also the corresponding judicial power of the Church—is born of the will and act by which Christ founded His Church. It remains true, however, that once the Church was constituted, as a perfect society, by the act of the Redeemer, not a few elements of resemblance to the structure of the civil society sprang from her very nature.

In one point, however, the fundamental difference between the two is particularly manifest. The establishment of the Church as a society was not effected from below, as was the case in the origin of the State, but from above; that is to say that Christ Who in His Church set up on earth the Kingdom of God which He had announced and destined for all men and all times, did not vest in the community of the faithful the mission of Master, Priest and Pastor which He had obtained from His Father for the salvation of mankind, but He transmitted and communicated it to a college of Apostles or messengers, selected by Himself, in order that they, by their preaching, by their priestly ministry, and by the social authority of their office, bring into the Church the multitude of the faithful to be sanctified, enlightened and led to the full maturity of followers of Christ. . . .

Two principal conclusions are to be deduced from the statements which we have made:

1. In the Church—unlike the State—the primordial subject of power, the supreme judge, the highest court of appeal, is never the community of the faithful. There-

fore, in the Church, as founded by Christ, there does not exist and can not exist any popular tribunal or judicial power deriving from the people.

2. The question of the extent and scope of ecclesiastical power also presents itself in a manner different from that of State power. What is decisive for the Church in the first place is the will of Christ, Who could give her, according to His Wisdom and goodness, means or powers of greater or lesser extent but always the minimum which is necessarily required by her nature and purpose. The power of the Church embraces man entirely, both his internal and external life, in order to lead him to the attainment of his supernatural destiny, so that he is completely subject to the law of Christ, which the Church has been constituted by her Divine founder to guard and to execute both in the external forum and in that of conscience, the internal forum. Consequently this power is a full and perfect one, though far removed from that "totalitarianism" which neither admits nor recognizes due regard for the clear and inalienable dictates of a sound conscience and which does violence to the laws of individual and social life written in the hearts of men (*Rom. ii.15*). In fact the Church, wielding her power, does not aim to enslave the human person, but to assure its liberty and perfection, redeeming it from the deficiencies, errors, aberrations in spirit and in heart, which sooner or later always end in dishonor and servitude.

A SHORT BIBLIOGRAPHY

Baldwin, Marshall W., *The Medieval Church* (Ithaca, 1953).

—————— *The Medieval Papacy in Action* (New York, 1950).

Barry, William F., *The Papacy and Modern Times 1303-1870* (New York, 1911).

—————— *The Papal Monarchy from St. Gregory the Great to Boniface VIII, 590-1303* (New York, 1902).

Butler, Dom B. C., *The Church and Infallibility* (New York, 1954).

—————— *The Vatican Council,* 2 vols. (New York, 1930).

Chapman, John, *Studies in the Early Papacy* (London, 1928).

Cullmann, Oscar, *Peter, Disciple, Apostle, Martyr: Historical and Theological Study* (Philadelphia, 1952).

Ehler, Sidney Z., and John B. Morrall, *Church and State Through the Centuries* (Westminster, Md., 1952).

Fliche, A., and V. Martin, *Histoire de l'Église depuis les origines jusqu'à nos jours* [Most of the volumes in this great 24-volume work have been published. Vols. 1 and 2 have been translated into English] (New York, 1942).

Giles, E., *Documents Illustrating Papal Authority* (London, 1952).

Gilson, Etienne, *The Church Speaks to the Modern World: The Social Teachings of Leo XIII* (New York, 1954).

Hughes, Philip, *A History of the Church,* 3 vols. (New York, 1934-1947).

—————— *Pope Pius the Eleventh* (New York, 1937).

—————— *A Popular History of the Church* (New York, 1947).

—————— *The Reformation in England* (3 vols.).

Janelle, Pierre, *The Catholic Reformation* (Milwaukee, 1949).

Journet, Charles, *The Primacy of Peter* (Westminster, Md., 1954).

———— The Church of the Word Incarnate: Vol. I: The Apostolic Hierarchy (New York, 1955).

Lecler, Joseph, The Two Sovereignties (London, 1952).

Leman, A., The Church in Modern Times, 1447-1789 (London, 1929).

MacCaffrey, James, The History of the Church in the Nineteenth Century, 1789-1908 (St. Louis, 1915).

Mann, H. K., The Lives of the Popes in the Middle Ages, 18 vols. (London, 1906-1932).

Pastor, Ludwig von, History of the Popes: 1378-1799 (St. Louis, 1891-1953).

Premoli, A., Contemporary Church History: 1900-1925 (London, 1925).

Shannon, A. C., The Popes and Heresy In the Thirteenth Century (New York, 1949).

Stewart, John Hall, A Documentary Survey of the French Revolution (New York, 1951).

Sturzo, Luigi, Church and State (New York, 1929).

Tolerance and the Catholic: A Symposium. Translated by George Lamb (New York, 1955).

LIST OF THE POPES

The following official list is taken, with permission, from Angelo Mercati, "The New List of the Popes," Medieval Studies, IX (1947) 71-80. The antipopes are indented. The dates for the pontificates up to Pope Eleutherius (175-189) are not absolutely sure. Because in the present state of historical research there still remains some doubt as to lawful claims in a few cases—indicated by a question mark—we have not given a progressive numerotation to the popes.

St. Peter, Galilean, 29-64 or 67.
St. Linus, of Tuscany, 67-76.
St. Anacletus or Cletus, Roman, 76-88.
St. Clement, Roman, 88-97.
St. Evaristus, Greek, 97-105.
St. Alexander I, Roman, 105-115.
St. Sixtus I, Roman, 115-125.
St. Telesphorus, Greek, 125-136.
St. Hyginus, Greek, 136-140.
St. Pius I, of Aquileia, 140-155.
St. Anicetus, Syrian, 155-166.
St. Soter, of Campania, 166-175.
St. Eleutherius, of Nicopolis in Epirus, 175-189.
St. Victor I, African, 189-199.
St. Zephyrinus, Roman, 199-217.
St. Callistus I, Roman, 217-222.
   [St. Hippolytus, Roman, 217-235.]
St. Urban I, Roman, 222-230.
St. Pontianus, Roman, 230-235.
St. Anterus, Greek, 235-236.
St. Fabian, Roman, 236-250.
St. Cornelius, Roman, 251-253.
   [Novatian, Roman, 251.]
St. Lucius I, Roman, 253-254.
St. Stephen I, Roman, 254-257.
St. Sixtus II, Greek, 257-258.

St. Dionysius, place of origin unknown, 259-268.
St. Felix I, Roman, 269-274.
St. Eutychianus, of Luni, 275-283.
St. Caius, Dalmatian, 283-296.
St. Marcellinus, Roman, 296-304.
St. Marcellus I, Roman, 308-309.
St. Eusebius, Greek, 309 or 310.
St. Milziadus or Melchiadus, African, 311-314.
St. Sylvester I, Roman, 314-335.
St. Mark, Roman, 336.
St. Julius I, Roman, 337-352.
Liberius, Roman, 352-366.
   [Felix II, Roman, 355-365.]
St. Damasus I, Spaniard, 366-384.
   [Ursinus, 366-367.]
St. Siricius, Roman, 384-399.
St. Anastasius I, Roman, 399-401.
St. Innocent I of Albano, 401-417.
St. Zozimus, Greek, 417-418.
St. Boniface I, Roman, 418-422.
   [Eulalius, 418-419.]
St. Celestine I, of Campania, 422-432.
St. Sixtus III, Roman, 432-440.
St. Leo I, the Great, of Tuscany, 440-461.
St. Hilarus, Sardinian, 461-468.
St. Simplicius, of Tivoli, 468-483.
St. Felix III (II), Roman, 483-492.
St. Gelasius I, African, 492-496.
Anastasius II, Roman, 496-498.
St. Symmachus, Sardinian, 498-514.
   [Lawrence, 498, 501-505.]
St. Hormisdas, of Frosinone, 514-523.
St. John I, of Tuscany, 523-526.
St. Felix IV (III), of Samnium, 526-530.
Boniface II, Roman, 530-532.
  ? [Dioscorus, of Alexandria, 530.]
John II, Roman, 533-535.
St. Agapitus I, Roman, 535-536
St. Silverius, of Campania, 536-537.
Vigilius, Roman, 537-555.
Pelagius I, Roman, 556-561.
John III, Roman, 561-574.
Benedict I, Roman, 575-579.

Pelagius II, Roman, 579-590.
St. Gregory I, the Great, Roman, 590-604.
Sabinianus, of Blera in Tuscany, 604-606.
Boniface III, Roman, 607.
St. Boniface IV, of Marsi, 608-615.
St. Deusdedit or Adeodatus I, Roman, 615-618.
Boniface V, Neapolitan, 619-625.
Honorius I, of Campania, 625-638.
Severinus, Roman, 640.
John IV, Dalmatian, 640-642.
Theodore I, Greek, 642-649.
St. Martin I, of Todi, 649-655.
St. Eugene I, Roman, 654-657.
St. Vitalian, of Segni, 657-672.
Adeodatus II, Roman, 672-676.
Donus, Roman, 676-678.
St. Agatho, Sicilian, 678-681.
St. Leo II, Sicilian, 682-683.
St. Benedict II, Roman, 684-685.
John V, Syrian, 685-686.
Cono, place of origin unknown, 686-687.
      [Theodore, 687.]
      [Paschal, 687.]
St. Sergius I, Syrian, 687-701.
John VI, Greek, 701-705.
John VII, Greek, 705-707.
Sisinnius, Syrian, 708.
Constantine, Syrian, 708-715.
St. Gregory II, Roman, 715-731.
St. Gregory III, Syrian, 731-741.
St. Zachary, Greek, 741-752.
Stephen II, Roman, 752.
Stephen III, Roman, 752-757.
St. Paul I, Roman, IV, 757-767.
      [Constantine, of Nepi, 767-769.]
      [Philip, 768.]
Stephen IV, Sicilian, 768-772.
Adrian I, Roman, 772-795.
St. Leo III, Roman, 795-816.
Stephen V, Roman, 816-817.
St. Paschal I, Roman, 817-824.
Eugene II, Roman, 824-827.
Valentine, Roman, 827.

Gregory IV, Roman, 827-844.
   [John, 844.]
Sergius II, Roman, 844-847.
St. Leo IV, Roman, 847-855.
Benedict III, Roman, 855-858.
   [Anastasius, the Librarian, 855.]
St. Nicholas I, the Great, Roman, 858-867.
Adrian II, Roman, 867-872.
John VIII, Roman, 872-882.
Marinus I, of Gallese, 882-884.
St. Adrian III, Roman, 884-885.
Stephen VI, Roman, 885-891.
Formosus, Bishop of Porto, 891-896.
Boniface VI, Roman, 896.
Stephen VII, Roman, 896-897
Romanus, of Gallese, 897.
Theodore II, Roman, 897.
John IX, of Tivoli, 898-900.
Benedict IV, Roman, 900-903.
Leo V, of Ardea, 903.
   [Christopher, Roman, 903-904.]
Sergius III, Roman, 904-911.
Anastasius III, Roman, 911-913.
Lando, of Sabina, 913-914.
John X, of Tossignano (Imola), 914-928.
Leo VI, Roman, 928.
Stephen VIII, Roman, 928-931.
John XI, Roman, 931-935.
Leo VII, Roman, 936-939.
Stephen IX, Roman, 939-942.
Marinus II, Roman, 942-946.
Agapitus II, Roman, 946-955.
John XII, Octavius, count of Tusculum, 955-964.
? Leo VIII, Roman, 963-965.
? Benedict V, Roman, 964-966.
John XIII, Roman, 965-972.
Benedict VI, Roman, 973-974.
   [Boniface VII, Roman, 974, 984-985.]
Benedict VII, Roman, 974-983.
John XIV, of Pavia, 983-984.
John XV, Roman, 985-996.
Gregory V, Saxon, 996-999.
   [John XVI, of Rossano, 997-998.]

Sylvester II, of Auvergne, (Gerbert), 999-1003.

John XVII, Roman, 1003.

John XVIII, Roman, 1004-1009.

Sergius IV, Roman, 1009-1012.

Benedict VIII, count of Tusculum, 1012-1024.
    [Gregory, 1012]

John XIX, count of Tusculum, 1024-1032.

Benedict IX, count of Tusculum, 1032-1044.

? Sylvester III, Roman, 1045

Benedict IX (for the second time), 1045.

? Gregory VI, Roman, 1045-1046.

? Clement II, of Saxony, 1046-1047.

Benedict IX (for the third time), 1047-1048.

Damasus II, Bavarian, 1048.

St. Leo IX, Bruno, count of Egisheim-Dagsburg, 1049-
    1054.

Victor II, Gebhard, count of Dollnstein-Hirschberg,
    1055-1057.

Stephen X, Frederick, Duke of Lorraine, 1057-1058.
    [Benedict X, Roman, 1058-1059.]

Nicholas II, of Burgundy, 1059-1061.

Alexander II, Milan, 1061-1073.
    [Honorius II, of Verona, 1061-1072.]

St. Gregory VII, of Tuscany, 1073-1075.
    [Clement III, of Parma, 1080, 1084-1100.]

Bl. Victor III, of Benevento, 1086-1087.

Bl. Urban II, French, 1088-1099.

Paschal II, of Ravenna, 1099-1118.
    [Theodoric, Bishop of St. Rufina, 1100.]
    [Albert, Bishop of Sabina, 1102.]
    [Sylvester IV, Roman, 1105-1111.]

Gelasius II, of Gaeta, 1118-1119.
    [Gregory VIII, French, 1118-1121.]

Callistus II, of Burgundy, 1119-1124.

Honorius II, of Fiagnano, 1124-1130.
    [Celestine II, Roman, 1124.]

Innocent II, Roman, 1130-1143.
    [Anacletus II, Roman, 1130-1138.]
    [Victor IV, 1138.]

Celestine II, of Castello, 1143-1144.

Lucius II, of Bologna, 1144-1145.

Bl. Eugene III, of Pisa, 1145-1153.

Anastasius IV, Roman, 1153-1154.

Adrian IV, English, 1154-1159.
Alexander III, of Siena, 1159-1181.
   [Victor IV, of Monticello, Tivoli, 1159-1164.]
   [Paschal III, 1164-1168.]
   [Callistus III, of Arezzo, 1168-1178.]
   [Innocent III, of Sezze, 1179-1180.]
Lucius III, of Lucca, 1181-1185.
Urban III, of Milan, 1185-1187.
Gregory VIII, of Benevento, 1187.
Clement III, Roman, 1187-1191.
Celestine III, Roman, 1191-1198.
Innocent III, of Anagni, 1198-1216.
Honorius III, Roman, 1216-1227.
Gregory IX, of Anagni, 1227-1241.
Celestine IV, of Milan, 1241.
Innocent IV, of Genoa, 1243-1254.
Alexander IV, of Anagni, 1254-1261.
Urban IV, of Troyes, 1261-1264.
Clement IV, French, 1265-1268.
Bl. Gregory X, of Piacenza, 1272-1276.
Bl. Innocent V, of Savoy, 1276.
Adrian V, of Genoa, 1276.
John XXI, Portuguese, 1276-1277.
Nicholas III, Roman, 1277-1280.
Martin IV, French, 1281-1285.
Honorius IV, Roman, 1285-1287.
Nicholas IV, of Ascoli, 1288-1292.
St. Celestine V, of Isernia, 1294.
Boniface VIII, of Anagni, 1294-1303.
Bl. Benedict XI, of Treviso, 1303-1304.
Clement V, French, 1305-1314.
John XXII, of Cahors, 1316-1334.
   [Nicholas V, of Corvaro, 1328-1330.]
Benedict XII, French, 1334-1342.
Clement VI, French, 1342-1352.
Innocent VI, French, 1352-1362.
Bl. Urban V, 1362-1370.
Gregory XI, French, 1370-1378.
Urban VI, Neapolitan, 1378-1389.
Boniface IX, Neapolitan, 1389-1404.
Innocent VII, of Sulmona, 1404-1406.
Gregory XII, Venetian, 1406-1415.
   [Clement VII, of Geneva, 1378-1394.]

[Benedict XIII, of Aragon, 1394-1423.]
[Alexander V, of Crete, 1409-1410.]
[John XXIII, Neapolitan, 1410-1415.]
Martin V, Roman, 1417-1431.
Eugene IV, Venetian, 1431-1447.
[Felix V, of Savoy, 1439-1449.]
Nicholas V, of Sarzana, 1447-1455.
Callistus III, of Valencia, 1455-1458.
Pius II, of Siena, 1458-1464.
Paul II, Venetian, 1464-1471.
Sixtus IV, of Savona, 1471-1484.
Innocent VIII, of Genoa, 1484-1492.
Alexander VI, of Valencia, 1492-1503.
Pius III, of Siena, 1503.
Julius II, of Savona, 1503-1513.
Leo X, Florentine, 1513-1521.
Adrian VI, of Utrecht, 1522-1523.
Clement VII, Florentine, 1523-1534.
Paul III, Roman, 1534-1549.
Julius III, Roman, 1550-1555.
Marcellus II, of Montepulciano, 1555.
Paul IV, Neapolitan, 1555-1559.
Pius IV, of Milan, 1559-1565.
St. Pius V, of Alessandria, 1566-1572.
Gregory XIII, of Bologna, 1572-1585.
Sixtus V, of Grottammare, 1585-1590.
Urban VII, Roman, 1590.
Gregory XIV, of Cremona, 1590-1591.
Innocent IX, of Bologna, 1591.
Clement VIII, Florentine, 1592-1605.
Leo XI, Florentine, 1605.
Paul V, Roman, 1605-1621.
Gregory XV, of Bologna, 1621-1623.
Urban VIII, Florentine, 1623-1644.
Innocent X, Roman, 1644-1655.
Alexander VII, of Siena, 1655-1667.
Clement IX, of Pistoia, 1667-1669.
Clement X, Roman, 1670-1676.
Innocent XI, of Como, 1676-1689.
Alexander VIII, Venetian, 1689-1691.
Innocent XII, Neapolitan, 1691-1700.
Clement XI, of Urbino, 1700-1721.
Innocent XIII, Roman, 1721-1724.

Benedict XIII, Roman, 1724-1730.
Clement XII, Florentine, 1730-1740.
Benedict XIV, of Bologna, 1740-1758.
Clement XIII, Venetian, 1758-1769.
Clement XIV, of Rimini, 1769-1774.
Pius VI, of Cesena, 1775-1799.
Pius VII, of Cesena, 1800-1823.
Leo XII, of Genga, 1823-1829.
Pius VIII, of Cingoli, 1829-1830.
Gregory XVI, of Belluno, 1831-1846.
Pius IX, of Senigallia, 1846-1878.
Leo XIII, of Carpineto, 1878-1903.
St. Pius X, of Riese, 1903-1914.
Benedict XV, of Genoa, 1914-1922.
Pius XI, of Desio, 1922-1939.
Pius XII, Roman, 1939-

INDEX

192